RED-
MAMAS

To Debbie & The book club

Read This and laugh — we women
are all totally nuts But Fun!!
Stay happy, healthy and keep laughing!

Best wishes —

Other Books by Jan King

When You're Hot, You're Hot:
How I Laughed My Way Through Menopause

It's a Mom Thing

It's a Girl Thing

RED-HOT MAMAS

Setting the World on Fire

JAN KING

**Andrews McMeel
Publishing**

Kansas City

03 04 05 06 07 EBI 10 9 8 7 6 5 4 3 2 1

Library of Congress Cataloging-in-Publication Data

King, Jan.
  Red-hot mamas : setting the world on fire / Jan King.
    p. cm.
  ISBN 0-7407-3845-3
    1. Women—Humor. I. Title: Setting the world on fire. II. Title.

PN6231.W6K58 2003
814'.54—dc21   2003050237

COVER PHOTO
Hair: Carolyn Carroll
Makeup: Jus' Judy
Nails: Marla Burgess
Photo: Charles William Bush

Book design by Holly Camerlinck

Attention: Schools and Businesses
Andrews McMeel books are available at quantity discounts with bulk purchase for educational, business, or sales promotional use. For information, please write to: Special Sales Department, Andrews McMeel Publishing, 4520 Main Street, Kansas City, Missouri 64111.

To my new best friends,
the Red-Hot Mamas from Arlington:
Carol Adams
Suzy Broyhill
Donetta Duncan
Mary Lunger
Catherine McNair
Susan Reed

CONTENTS

ACKNOWLEDGMENTS

To my editor, Kelly Gilbert.
Thank you, thank you, thank you.
Thank you for helping me to become a better writer with each book.
Thank you for always understanding where a woman
of my advanced age is coming from.
Thank you for always calling me back.

INTRODUCTION

Hey, girlfriends. Don't put those electric fans away in storage just yet. Rumor has it that as we get older, we gals get hotter. Even us postmenopausal boomers are still setting the world on fire. Contrary to popular opinion, we have not crashed and burned. In fact, we're lookin' pretty good. Our bodies are still hot—even if it's hormonally induced. So what? Estrogen is our fuel of choice.

In *Red-Hot Mamas*, I'm going to talk about how women are able to make their lives so memorable. We are endlessly fascinating creatures with the singular ability to operate on multilevels. Who else can drive a car, drink a Starbucks low-fat latte, polish our nails, talk on the cell phone, and listen to Dr. Laura all at the same time? Not any man out there, that's for sure.

No matter what decade of life we're in—twenties, thirties, forties, and up—women are always doing something really cool. And whatever that is, we make it look good. *Red-Hot Mamas* shamelessly exposes our favorite female activities and proves that we gals can find humor in anything from shopping to surgery.

What's more, women are the only living organisms capable of:

* Understanding the difference between eggshell, ecru, and beige
* Spending the entire day with a girlfriend, then calling her on the cell phone the minute she gets home
* Experiencing pure joy, sitting through a two-hour chick-flick, sobbing our eyes out

✻ Requiring a twelve-step program to throw away one lipstick

In the new millennium, women have finally come into their own. We have made important breakthroughs not only with our brains, but with our other organs, too. Take the vagina, for instance. For years it was ranked below the gall bladder and pancreas in popularity. But now, thanks to Eve Ensler's *Vagina Monologues*, the vagina has not only come out of the closet, it's talking all over the country. In fact, you can't shut it up. The injustices, the discrimination, the abuse—blah, blah, blah. But that's okay. It's a little organ with a big agenda.

And speaking of agendas, *Red-Hot Mamas* will discuss what we females typically do with our lives. The marathon shopping trips, the three-hour lunches, the religion of the beauty salon—all the stuff that really floats our boats. This book will explain why we get such joy out of our compulsive behavior. It will also provide answers to important psychological questions you've been wondering about for years. Questions like: "Am I completely nuts, or do all women act this way?"

When you realize you're not alone, you're going to feel better about yourself than you have in years. You can stop calling your shrink ten times a day to ask if you are an obsessive-compulsive. Accept it. Enjoy it. Wallow in it. Go out and set the world on fire!

ONE

Fast Girls: Sex and the Suburbs

I may not be a spring chicken anymore, but honestly, do I have to be reminded of it every two seconds? Every time I turn on the TV, the commercials show women my age engaged in the following activities:

* Sitting on a bench at their kids' soccer games, suffering with hemorrhoids
* Caught in traffic, worrying about bladder control
* Scrubbing stains out of their dentures
* Advising each other they don't have that "fresh smell"
* Doing the tango in adult diapers

Is this depressing or what? Nowadays, a healthy, happy woman over forty is harder to find than the plot of a David Lynch movie. And if it isn't bad enough to feel old and smelly, now there's a TV show that makes us feel completely inadequate sexually. It's called *Sex and the City*. And it's—surprise—about the adventures of four single, attractive women living in New York City. All of the gals juggle boyfriends[1] and great careers. They go to chic bars where

---

1. From their beds.

they pick up men by the busload. By today's standards,[2] they're considered role models for women. Oh, really? Did I mention that they are also psycho-bitch-amoral-nymphomaniacs?

At any given moment, these gals are having so much sex, they need to install speed bumps outside their bedroom doors. They haven't got a clue as to the difference between right and wrong . . . between right and left—that's another story. But I guess the audience doesn't see it that way because the girls live in New York, where anything obscene is called "sophisticated." What I want to know is when do they actually work at their jobs? After one of their "sophisticated" evenings, they'd need at least three days of recovery in intensive care.

This is *so* not what "working girls" were in my day. When I was a single, working gal, I actually had a job. I was a high school teacher at South Philadelphia High School. Yo, Adrian. And believe me, the only wild sex going on around me was in my classroom, between the students. Even if I had the inclination to bed down every guy named Tony in South Philly,[3] where could I find the time? I taught biology classes from 8 A.M. until 4 P.M. Then at night, I took graduate education classes at the University of Pennsylvania.

By the time I got back to my apartment at 9 P.M., I was exhausted. I'd pop a gourmet TV dinner into the oven, grade papers, and go to bed. If I had tried to follow the racy footsteps of Miranda or Carrie, I wouldn't have been able to get up off my chair and walk to the blackboard.[4]

You know, when I stop and think about it, the premise of *Sex and the City* is nothing but a total fantasy. I've never known any woman who had either the time, the freedom, or the stamina to enjoy that kind of wanton, nonstop sex. And I lived through the '60s. That's saying something.[5] When I was growing up, there was definitely a

2. Or substandards.
3. 750,000 of them.
4. Without the help of industrial strength Astroglide.
5. That I am really, really old.

vast right-wing conspiracy[6] that kept me from losing my virginity. Here's a brief chronology of those opposing forces:

HIGH SCHOOL YEARS

My Dad—The man had one career goal in life: to keep me a virgin until I got married. As the self-appointed head of his Virgin Task Force, he established a rigid code of ethics I had to follow.

Any infraction of it carried the punishment of life imprisonment in my room. And there were no plea bargains available, either. God forbid I came home from a date displaying any of these telltale signs:

* A hickey
* Skirt on backward
* Smeared lipstick
* Baggy panty hose
* Beard burns
* Rug burns[7]

My Priest—Growing up Catholic in the '50s and '60s was a better deterrent to sex than watching a woman give birth without anesthesia. In order to keep me a chaste Catholic girl, my dad forced me to go to confession every Saturday afternoon. I had to confess everything I had done all week, including the sins of the flesh. Not the best way to get in the mood for a Saturday night date, huh? Having to do this could kill the libido of Julio Iglesias. Trust me, it was torture. I'd stand there in the confessional line, quaking in my boots, waiting for my turn to be grilled like an Oscar Mayer hot dog.

Confessing a tongue kiss would get you ten Our Fathers, ten Hail Marys, and a stern lecture about the evils of temptation. Petting

6. Spearheaded by Hillary Clinton.
7. Automatic death penalty.

was far worse. The priest would deliver a sermon about your promiscuity at one hundred decibels that was heard by everyone in the church. Your friends would pull out their loose-leafs and take notes on what you did. The penance for petting was an entire rosary plus the threat of having your soul remain in purgatory for half of eternity.

But if anybody ever dared confess to the "wild thing"—oh-oh. The confession booth would shake from the priest's roar. Then before he let you leave, he made a public announcement that your immortal soul was damned to burn in hell for eternity. Then he'd add, "Have a nice day."

Bras and Girdles—Looking back, I am convinced that the manufacturers of bras and girdles of the '50s and '60s were actually secret agents of the Catholic Church. Why? Because once my private parts were ensconced in this Cold-War armor, there was no way a guy was going to get through to them. In those days, bras and girdles were made from space-age materials like neoprene, Tupperware, and Formica. Trust me: Your chances of fooling around were nada. I practically had to enlist the Jaws of Life to get my girdle off at the end of the day.

The bras had dozens of metal hooks and eyes sewn up the back. There was never enough time, even on a 3 A.M. prom night, for a boy to unhook all of those babies. Foreplay was literally unheard of until the '70s, when women stopped wearing bras and started burning them.

COLLEGE

The Housemother—College used to be the most common time for a girl to shed her cumbersome virginity. However, back in the '60s, that was harder to do than making a 4.0 average. This was because the Virgin Task Force, once headed by our dads, was taken over by the world's most formidable Feminazi, the housemother. She ruled the dorm with an iron will as well as an iron corset. What a tyrant! Women prisoners at Rikers had more freedom than we did. She corralled us vestal virgins within her walls, and our virginity was guaranteed by these dictates she posted on the front door:

1. Any couple caught kissing at the front door will be publicly hosed down like a dog in heat.
2. All ovulating coeds will automatically be placed under house arrest for a period of twenty-four hours.
3. Chaperones at all parties must be over sixty-five years of age and belong to the order of the Sisters of Chastity.
4. Any man found in a coed's room will automatically be expelled, then chemically castrated.
5. Any girl caught sneaking in after curfew will be blindfolded and shot by the ROTC firing squad.

What's a girl to do? We all had the itch but we weren't allowed to scratch it. So we graduated with the seemingly impossible odds of keeping 3.5 averages and our virginity.

MARRIAGE

No matter what your age, the following holds true for all women: We only get a few years in our lives when we are totally free to enjoy a lot of recreational sex. So enjoy yourselves. It's later than you think. There's always a price to pay later on. But this time it wasn't our dads, priests, or housemothers who put the kibosh on our fun. Ironically, it was the product of that fun—yep, the kids. After the first child came along, I never had five free minutes again. It was enough to drive me nuts. You remember Angelina Jolie in *Girl, Interrupted*? Well, she wasn't half as nutty as a mom interrupted.

For the next ten years, my husband and I were never able to complete a sexual experience in our bedroom. After the kids arrived, our bedroom became public domain. It was no longer a sanctuary for husband and wife, it was a sanctuary for wildlife. Our bedroom served the following purpose for our kids:

Babies to toddlers: sleep in bed with us

Ages 4–5: stand outside our bedroom door and cry

Ages 5–9: barge into our bedroom unannounced, even when the door was closed

Ages 10–13: fight outside our bedroom door

Ages 13–18: stand outside our bedroom door and call us from their cell phones

Once we figured this out, we learned how to do it in three minutes or less. Where do you think the "quickie" started?

MIDDLE AGE

Hormone Hiatus—By fifty, hopefully, we've gotten rid of our kids, our pets, and our sexual hang-ups. This should be the time when we're raring to go. But wait. We've got a teeny-weeny problem. Our hormone levels are dropping faster than the Dow Jones. Our sex drives have been declared officially dead. We should probably post a DNR sign on our lower extremities. Am I making myself clear or do I have to act it out with a sock puppet? Nowadays, when we get into bed, we don't have sex on our minds. So when our husbands request it, we have to come up with more excuses than Gary Condit at a Senate investigation. Here are just a few things that we'd rather be doing than having a roll in the hay:

* Listen to Jay Leno's monologue
* Read Danielle Steele's latest tearjerker
* Tweeze our eyebrows
* Do the *New York Times* crossword
* Watch other people have sex on Showtime

So there you have it. This is the way our generation grew up. Wow. It's truly amazing that the population grew at all during those decades. Come to think of it, that was when the concept of ZPG originated. Luckily, the population made a comeback during the past ten years after the advent of Starbucks and Showtime Adult Features.

Sex and the Suburbs

1. The correct definition of a bisexual woman is a person who:
   a. has sex with both genders
   b. suffers from gender confusion
   c. has both male and female sex organs
   d. has sex twice a year

2. The clinical difference between a young lover and a husband is:
   a. 45 years
   b. 45 pounds
   c. 45 chromosomes
   d. 45 minutes

3. What price does a man have to pay when he is caught talking dirty to another woman?
   a. his marriage
   b. never-ending guilt
   c. marriage counseling
   d. $9.99 a minute

4. What is the name of the condition that paralyzes women from the waist down?
   a. M.S.
   b. A.L.S.
   c. Gullain Barre
   d. marriage

5. Statistically, men prefer virgins because:
   a. of an Oedipal complex
   b. it's an ego booster
   c. they fear sexual diseases
   d. they can't take criticism

6. Women experience which type of orgasm 98 percent of the time?
   a. vaginal
   b. clitoral
   c. multiple
   d. faked

7. Most men cannot tell when a woman has an orgasm because they:
   a. don't pay attention
   b. don't know the clinical signs
   c. don't really care
   d. are never around when it happens

The answers to all of the above are d, as in "don't touch me."

Scoring:
1–3 correct: Try harder.
4–7 correct: Just fake it.

TWO

Cosmetic Surgery:
In Your Face

Three years ago, I noticed my trusty Canon Elph camera had started to take bad pictures. I remember thinking there must be a problem with the lens, because my face looked wider and a bit out of focus. My eyes also looked a little puffy and blurry in all the pictures. Well, duuuh. Obviously, I was not connecting all the dots here. Instead, I was off taking another cruise on DeNile. The only thing that was out of focus was my brain.

Somehow, I never thought the aging process was going to get around to me. But unlike Dorian Gray, my pictures were aging. That's when I started to warm up to the idea of having a face-lift. Actually, more than just warming up—I was burning up with desire! However, there's nothing that cools you off faster than listening to other people's opinions. My first mistake was asking advice from my family and friends. Bad idea. The things they said were completely motivated by their own agendas.

MY HUSBAND

He Said: "Honey, you don't need it! You still look like my beautiful bride."

He Really Thought: "Omigod! This is going to set me back twenty grand. I'll never be able to afford a doctor again. I won't be able to retire until I'm eighty-five and dragging around a prostate as big as a house."

MY BEST GIRLFRIEND

She Said: "A face-lift? You can't be serious. Why would you put yourself through that ordeal when you look so young and beautiful?"

She Really Thought: "Oh-oh. Right now she looks at least ten years older than me. But if she goes for this, I'm going to look like her mother."

MY SON

He Said: "Mom—no way! I'll end up with a mother who looks like Cher."

He Really Thought: "Bummer, dude. Forget about a new car and grad school. I'll have to ride the bus and flip burgers at Mickey D's for the next four years."

The bottom line is simple. Take it from one who's been there, done that. Don't ask anybody. It's your decision to put your best face forward—even though it may be a different one every few years.

My next step was to have a consultation with a cosmetic surgeon. I asked three of my doctors at Cedars-Sinai who they thought was the best in L.A. They unanimously said, "Dr. Alfred Cohen." So Cohen it was. He's the man. I called his office and they couldn't have been nicer. His receptionist, Barbara, said the consultation fee was $100. If I decided to go ahead with the surgery, it would be applied toward my total cost. I figured that would get me .0001 of an eyelid. But what the heck.

Dr. Cohen's office was impressive. The reception area was a combo of polished black marble with stunning white orchid plants placed artistically all over the room. The staff was wonderful. When I was ushered into Dr. Cohen's office, I felt like I had stepped into the pages of *Architectural Digest*. It was done in white and ecru fabric, contrasted with black lacquer furniture. Stunning! Total perfection. It was like gazing at pristine, new-fallen snow. There was absolutely nothing out of place. Not one item to straighten, wipe off, or rearrange. An obsessive-compulsive would have to kill himself right on the spot.

Dr. Cohen was the epitome of perfection in his white lab coat, Gucci silk tie, and dental school–perfect teeth. There was a family portrait hanging on the wall, and I noticed even his shar-pei didn't have wrinkles.[1] Dr. Cohen was soft-spoken and calm. Just being around him produced the same effect as three cups of chamomile tea.

He took a brief medical history. We discussed the successful breast cancer surgery and recovery I made three years earlier. If I decided to go ahead with the surgery, I would need to have my internist examine me, do a chest X ray, and get specific blood tests.

Then he talked at length about the technical aspect of the surgical procedures. Blah, blah, blah. That part was boring. I wanted to get right down to the good part . . . moi. The kisser. I was thinking, "Come on, Dr. Cohen—tell me the part about how young I'm going to look!" That's when he began explaining what the surgery would do to correct the "aging process." When he said that keyword, "aging," I knew we had gotten to the good part. That's when he started talking in politically correct–speak. There was no way he was going to mention X-rated words like sags, bags, crepey skin, or jowls. All those nasty terms were replaced by the kinder and gentler term, "aging." As in "I will make an incision here . . . in this area of aging." With that, he pointed to my jowls, which were drooping more than J. Edgar Hoover's.[2]

He said he would remove the excess skin on my upper and lower

1. Botox injections.
2. Or Richard M. Nixon's—a toss-up.

eyelids. This is called a blepharoplasty. Also, he'd tighten the skin around my jaw line and smooth out the labio-facial folds through a mid-lift, technically called a rhydidectomy. Most of the incisions would be hidden in my hairline. After hearing those terms, one thing was certain. I needed an interpreter. As far as I knew, I didn't have a blephero or a rhydid. The only part I recognized was labia, and that made me nervous. How could he tell I needed that tightened, too?

Next came the "magic touch." This occurred when the doctor stood behind me and smoothed back my face with the palms of his hands. This showed me the look he expected to achieve. I gazed into the mirror at a face that looked like mine, only twenty years younger. That did it. I was sold, lock, stock, and barrel. If he said, "The procedure will cost five million dollars," I would have said, "No problem—I'll go out and heist a Brink's truck."

"You will look very well rested," he said. I thought, "Oh yeah? Wait a minute, here. This could be the deal breaker. When I'm paying a small fortune, I expect to look twenty years younger. If I want to look well rested, I'll stay in bed for a week."

But then the scalpel turned—big time. I was taken into another room where the nurse took pictures of my face from all angles. Side view, full facial nudity, you name it. The clincher came when Dr. Cohen fanned my photos out on his desk, like Miss Cleo does with her tarot cards. Mercy! I looked like the Bride of Frankenstein on a bad-hair day. After taking a good look at myself in the unforgiving light of those Polaroids, I almost screamed, "Prep me for surgery—stat!"

Somehow, I managed not to faint, scream, or ask for a Depend. That happened when I went into the financial manager's office to discuss the costs. You know the drill. The doctors, themselves, never discuss that dirty business. They figure one shock is enough— when they have to break the news you actually need their services. So they pay a really attractive woman to deliver the second shock for them. His beautiful financial manager had the pleasure of delivering the spark that set fire to my husband's wallet.

I signed all the papers and picked my date, October 30. It might be a real hoot to appear at my door, bruised and bandaged, sending the trick-or-treaters screaming into the night! However, Barbara said that Dr. Cohen likes his patients to spend at least two nights at a cosmetic recovery spa. She produced some brochures of this fabbo place called the Hidden Garden. Now she had my full attention. The place looked like the Ritz-Carlton.[3]

Nowadays, cosmetic surgeons feel that if you go right home after surgery, no matter what your intentions, you'll be doing too much. This contributes to more swelling and bruising. In my case, I knew he was right. Cosmetic surgery patients get no sympathy. My husband would probably have me up on a ladder installing a new roof. At the Hidden Garden, there would be nurses around the clock to bring ice packs for my eyes, dispense my meds, and baby me in every way. I chose the Paper White Suite from the pictures in the brochure. It had this yummy huge, lacy bed, lace draperies at shuttered windows, and a big, white, overstuffed sofa. Plus I couldn't resist the darling stuffed bunnies placed all over the room. The thought of lounging there in a big, comfy bed, with all my meals served on a white wicker tray complete with the de rigueur bud vase was just too much. I caved in and signed up for four days. Pricey? You bet! But, what the heck. I was feeling better than I had in years. My husband, on the other hand, was having a heart attack.

After the consultation, I was floating on cloud nine. I called all my girlfriends to tell them I was going to do it! Mistake #2. Remember the song "Hey, You, Get Off of My Cloud"? Yeah? Well, now you've got the picture. Don't listen to your friends before contemplating surgery. Even though they are well-intentioned, you'll

---

3. With a bruised clientele.

be subjected to stories more horrifying than a Thomas Harris novel. Here are just a few:

* "I watched a surgeon do a face-lift on the Discovery Channel. Oh my God! They peel your skin back like an orange, then cut through all this muscle. It's horrifying! I almost threw up."
* "My mother's friend had a face-lift last year and she's still taking pain medication. Poor thing. She hasn't smiled in over a year."
* "My sister just had a face-lift. She threw up for twenty-four hours after surgery and busted out her stitches. She said it was worse than going through labor."
* "My girlfriend went to this doctor who promised she'd look ten years younger. But instead, she just looks surprised all the time."

Thanks for sharing.

DOS (DAY OF SURGERY)

Truthfully, the worst part was the hour I spent just before surgery. I had to arrive by 7 A.M., which for me is like the middle of the night. The nurse took me into the pre-op room, where I was instructed to take everything off and put on a surgical gown. I also had to put on surgical stockings. They looked exactly like the kind my Croatian grandmother used to wear every day. Boy, was I a sight. I sat there in this freezing cold cubicle waiting for the doctor and nurses to come get me. It took roughly 1.3 centuries.

I signed the release form, you know, the one that says if your mouth ends up in the middle of your forehead it's not their fault. Then the anesthesiologist came in and explained what he was going to do. Finally, Dr. Cohen appeared, wearing his scrubs. He briefly went over the procedures again. Everybody was serious and businesslike. Oh-oh. I needed warm fuzzies. I wanted to be back in the dreamy art deco office with the panoramic view of L.A. What happened to the white orchids and plush chairs? Geez Louise. The things I put myself through to look young.

The operating room could scare even George Clooney. It's pretty formidable. I sat upright on the operating table while Dr. Cohen outlined my eyes and neck with a surgical magic marker. He measured stuff and generally futzed around for ten minutes. When he was through, I must have looked like one of those posters showing a side of beef with the muscle groups mapped out.

I was relieved when they told me I could finally lie down. Then the nurse covered me with a heated blankie. Aaaah—that was wonderful. The anesthesiologist said he was going to start my IV drip, and the next thing was . . . lights out, baybee! I woke up in the recovery area three hours later. My head was bandaged in an elaborate pressure dressing. I felt like the giant disembodied head from *The Wizard of Oz*. It was weird. Nothing hurt but the two drains in the back of my head. Those were sore and driving me crazy. I got an overwhelming case of shpilkes, where I kept moving my legs to divert my attention from those drains.

The nurses said to lie still or I'd swell more. "Really?" I thought. "Well, if I can't move, my big swollen head is going to explode." But somehow, I managed to keep my legs completely still for the next three hours. I wondered if I could do that. But then it came to me. All I had to do was pretend I was making love. Piece of cake. I was counting the minutes until the nurse from the Hidden Garden would come for me. My nurse, a gal named Eddie, was a total pro. She deftly whisked me in my wheelchair out the back door into the rear elevator, making sure nobody saw me and my hideous bandaged head. The last thing a cosmetic surgeon wants is for one of his patients contemplating surgery to see one who had it looking like she just got run over by a Greyhound bus. Their OR schedule would be emptier than an Enron office.

When we arrived at the Hidden Garden, I was led up a flower-intensive path to my charming bungalow. Eddie tucked me into the fabulous white lacy king-sized bed. It was all toasty and heated up. I was in heaven! Within an hour, she brought me a tray of delicious-looking food, served on beautiful china. The food was cooked and pureed, because for the first time in my life, I had trouble opening my mouth to eat. But not to worry. I managed to suck in everything on the tray between clenched jaws. It was so delicious, I would have had them give it to me through an IV if necessary.

Each day, Eddie would drive me over to Dr. Cohen's office. The first day, I refused to look at myself in the mirror. But on the second day, I did. Surprise. It wasn't so bad at all. My eyelids were pink and swollen and there was bruising under each eye and on my neck, but it was minimal. The only really horrifying sight was my hair. It was coated with this orange antibacterial goop they put on it for surgery. They told me it was necessary because the incisions went into my hairline at the base of my skull and above my ears. But other than looking like an Irish setter who just had a flea-dip, I was already beginning to like what I saw.

POST-OP SCHEDULE

Day 1—Drains and post-op pressure dressing removed. Lighter dressing applied. Can move my head. It isn't severed from my body, after all. It only feels like it.

Day 2—Hideous orange goop on my hair washed off by Eddie at the Hidden Garden. Eddie is a goddess.

Day 3—Smaller stitches in front and back of ears removed. I'm looking less and less like Frankenstein every day. That's progress.

Day 10—All stitches and clips removed. What a relief! I won't inadvertently set off any security alarms now.

Day 14—Dr. Cohen treated me to a makeup session in Beverly Hills. I went out to dinner that night. Omigod! I was in love with the results already.

Three Weeks—I was able to start sleeping on my side again. Thank God, because I snore when I sleep on my back. My husband sent roses to Dr. Cohen.

Two Months—Just a few areas of numbness left in front of my ears, the back of my neck and under my chin. Okay, and my face feels a bit tight when I turn my head side to side, like there's glue on my skin. Otherwise, I feel perfect! Well, maybe a little weird, but I look so damn good, who cares?

In Your Face

1. You know you've had too much cosmetic surgery when you've had your face pulled up more times than:
   a. three
   b. the muscles can bear
   c. recommended
   d. Ted Kennedy's pants

2. After the initial consult for a face-lift, you should:
   a. take a second honeymoon
   b. have second thoughts
   c. seek a second opinion
   d. get a second mortgage

3. You have had too many face-lifts when your:
   a. skin loses all elasticity
   b. face looks pulled
   c. face has numb areas
   d. dog doesn't recognize you

4. An astute cosmetic surgeon can tell Joan Collins's age by:
   a. the number of blepheroplasties she's had
   b. the type of incisions the surgeons made
   c. looking at the skin on her neck
   d. carbon dating

5. You have had a bad face-lift when you chew and:
   a. it's painful
   b. your jaws feel numb
   c. your movement is restricted
   d. your eyebrows go up and down

6. Cardiac arrest associated with cosmetic surgery only happens:
   a. in .01 percent of cases
   b. if the patient had undetected heart disease
   c. once in a decade
   d. when opening the bill

7. Cosmetic surgery may be indicated when your photos need airbrushing:
   a. around the eyes
   b. to eliminate wrinkles
   c. 100 percent of the time
   d. with a caulking gun

The answers to all the above are d, as in "dermabrasion."

Scoring:

1–3 correct: Cosmetic surgery is elective.
4–7 correct: Face-lift indicated as emergency surgery.

THREE

$\mathcal{S}$tress $\mathcal{B}$usters:
Hit Me with Your Best Shot

Okay, it's a given. We all live in a high-powered world in which we constantly deal with stress. Our checkbooks are overdrawn. Our kids failed algebra. Our husbands' companies are downsizing. We just found our first gray hair.[1] Hey, we all have to cope. But the thing I find interesting is how men and women deal with stress in different ways.

Women usually deal with their problems and accompanying stress in one of three ways:

1. Talking their problems out with a therapist
2. Meditating
3. Eating three dozen Krispy Kremes

On the other hand, men relieve their stress by:

1. Watching even more football
2. Having more sex[2]

---

1. On our chests.
2. By themselves.

3. Doing nothing, hoping the problems will go away by themselves

These methods seem to provide temporary relief to some people, but none of them work well for me. Especially the ways men deal with stress. I don't get it. Football raises their blood pressure. Problems never go away by themselves. And having more sex? What's up with that? Forget it. At my age, sex can actually cause more stress than relieve it. Here are some solutions that work well for me:

STRESS BUSTER #1—I FOUND MY MOJO AT OJOMOH

I started going to Joseph Ojomoh's boxing classes over a year ago. In the beginning, we learned the punching techniques holding light weights. Then over the next several months, one by one, everyone traded in their weights for the real deal, i.e., boxing gloves. That was everyone but moi, your total pacifist wuss. Just the sight of those gloves freaked me out. I thought that once I started punching with the gloves, I'd develop biceps bigger than Popeye's.[3] I worried about tearing a tendon, breaking a finger, busting my spleen . . . blah, blah, blah. I had more excuses than the O.J. jury.

Then one day when I was in the sporting goods store, something strange happened. Like mythical Sirens, the Everlast boxing gloves on aisle six started calling out to me. Try me on . . . try me on. I was being lured into dangerous waters. I could almost hear the surf crashing over the rocks. Transfixed, I put on a pair of boxing gloves along with the regulation shorts. I was a woman possessed. The next thing I knew, I was at the cash register paying for them. Yep. I traded in my de la Rentas for De La Hoyas. Let's get ready to rumble.

The first time I wore my big, red Everlast gloves in class, Joseph started grinning from ear to ear. I know what he was thinking— the last virgin in the class finally gave it up! It was a red-letter

3. Or triceps bigger than Chynna's.

STRESS BUSTERS: HIT ME WITH YOUR BEST SHOT | 25

day.[4] Joseph is a sweetheart of a guy. But make no mistake. He's built like a Marine drill sergeant and runs his class like boot camp at Fort Bragg. He walks around the room wearing these huge gloves that look like catchers' mitts. He holds them up in front of our faces, and we lowly grunts punch into them. And here's the fun part. Even those big, massive steroidal-type guys who slam away into Joseph's mitts can't make him move a millimeter. The guy is Iron Man.

Within a nanosecond of my putting on gloves, Joseph is in my face with his mitts. He calls out, left . . . right . . . uppercut. The first punch—I'm scared to death. The second—I'm tentative. But by the third—watch out! Wow. I am transformed into Rocky. Eye of the tiger, baybee. Bam—bam—wham—bam! I zero in on the mitts and all I can see is the image of my husband's ex on one of them and my ex on the other. I have no mercy. No mas!

Joseph loves it. Here I am, this postmenopausal grandma, punching away at his mitts with all my might. Bam—this one's for all the heartache Plaintiff gave me about my alimony. Slam—this one is for all the telemarketers who ruin my dinner every night. Wham—this is for that moron at the credit card company who keeps charging me late fees I don't owe. Wow! This feels good. I'm a regular Mike Tyson. Watch out for your ears.

After what seems like an hour, Joseph steps back. I have this surreal feeling like I'm in a tunnel. I've been concentrating so hard on the target, I am near collapse, sweating, shoulders aching, gasping for breath. Torture? Heck no. I love it. I just beat the crap out of my worst nightmares. I feel totally empowered.

STRESS BUSTER #2: SHOP TILL YOU DROP

A shopping spree is, for me, the only way to release pent-up hostility without breaking major bones.[5] One of the biggest sources

---

4. Actually, a red-knuckle day.
5. Other people's.

of stress between my husband and me is that he spends every weekend golfing. It makes me crazy. There are a hundred things I'd like to plan for the weekends.[6] But instead, I end up alone and steamed. Talk about your abandonment issues! I could do a whole *Oprah* by myself.

So after some serious soul searching,[7] I decided that I was wasting my time getting mad. I figured I wouldn't get mad, I'd get even—at Nordstrom. Never has the phrase "When the going gets tough, the tough go shopping" had more meaning.

So while he's out there golfing, I am getting my revenge by being unfaithful. You heard me. I am having a ménage à trois with Donna Karan and Ralph Lauren. There's nothing like Ralph's soft leather pants and Donna's cashmere sweaters to help you get rid of your hostility.

I think of it as preventive medicine, like taking penicillin. In order to keep my immune system from crashing under fulminating resentment, I stock up on Ellen Tracy blazers, Guess jeans, pashmina shawls, and Coach bags. You know—the necessities of life. It's a quick fix and makes you feel better than all the Xanax in Liza Minnelli's medicine cabinet. There's no better therapy than plunking down sixty bucks on a lacy La Perla bra and exquisite Wofford stockings. Trust me. A pair of $300 Jimmy Choo slingbacks will dampen the flames of anger faster than all the water at Seaworld.

STRESS BUSTER #3— THE LIFETIME MOVIE SOBFEST

There are those times when it all gets to be just too much. My husband and I are butting heads about money, the kids, or the exes.

---

6. He could wash windows, rake leaves, clean gutters.
7. And a trip to the ATM.

What else is there? During these times when I feel life has become a battleground, all I want to do is escape. Unfortunately, I can't just hop on a plane and relax at a fabulous spa like La Costa. Heck, I can't even afford a weekend at Motel 6 watching the six-year-old videos from a vibrating bed.[8]

So what do I do to escape the turmoil? I'll tell you what I do. Since I rarely drink, I don't get wasted for the weekend. Instead, I indulge myself in a "lost weekend" of another sort. The kind with Sara Lee. It begins on Friday night when I shower, put on my softest pj's, and crawl into my big, comfy bed. But before crawling in, I make sure I have the following items:

1. Three boxes of Kleenex
2. One quart of Häagen-Daz—praline pecan
3. A Sara Lee cheesecake
4. A large bag of M&M's
5. A 64-ounce bottle of Diet Pepsi[9]

Then I tune into the Lifetime movie channel and leave it on nonstop until Sunday afternoon. For me, there is nothing like having a giant emotional catharsis, along with Donna Mills, Joanna Kerns, and Patty Duke. Nothing makes me feel better about my own problems than watching a story about someone else's miserable, tortured life. Even our biggest battles seem like *Sesame Street* compared to these story lines:

1. Joanna Kerns losing custody of her three kids (all under six) to her evil, manipulative lawyer ex-husband who plotted against her with his floozy lover.[10]
2. Donna Mills getting beat up in her kitchen by her psychotic boyfriend because she burned his toast.

---

8. Not after that last shopping spree.
9. We must watch our calories.
10. Who is also her best friend.

3. Patty Duke simultaneously suffering from five life-threatening illnesses and conquering them all, only to die from injuries suffered during a freak skateboard accident.

4. Kate Jackson having her baby stolen from its crib by some deranged nurse's aide.

5. Lindsey Wagner losing five husbands in five years from "natural causes."

Talk about your drama queens. This channel rules. Nobody does it better. Here's how my weekend goes. I feed my face, cry, blow my nose a dozen times, then rehydrate with Diet Pepsi. Repeat. Repeat again. As easy as shampooing. After the first twenty-four hours of this behavior, I am able to get rid of any emotional baggage I'm carrying.[11] Thirty-six hours of this kind of emotional wrenching positively eliminates all my demons. Too bad Linda Blair didn't know about this technique before they called in the exorcist.

STRESS BUSTER #4 — THE SPRINGER FREE-FOR-ALL

There have been times when I was so exhausted from fighting the daily battles, I had no energy left to work off my hostilities through exercise. This is why the Jerry Springer show provides such a wonderful public service. It offers high-quality, low-class head butting that can be enjoyed vicariously from the comfort of my own couch. There is absolutely no connubial beef they haven't aired and exploited for public consumption.

Within minutes, I am totally sucked in. There are always issues I can identify with. I also improve my communication skills by listening to their high-caliber debates.[12] Who wouldn't take ghoulish delight in the slug-fests where some three-hundred-pound woman

---

11. More than FedEx.
12. "You bleep, bleep, bleepin' bleep."

beats her abusive husband with her hair extensions? But the real bonus is that after watching these troglodytes go at it for an hour, my domestic situation doesn't seem half as bad as before. Even my husband is looking pretty darn good.

Hit Me with Your Best Shot

1. Being outdoors has a calming effect on the nerves. The best natural way to soothe upsets is by:
   a. cutting the grass
   b. smelling freshly cut grass
   c. lying in the grass
   d. smoking grass

2. Which actress was brilliantly cast in a Lifetime movie in the role of Mother Teresa?
   a. Meryl Streep
   b. Dame Judi Dench
   c. Maggie Smith
   d. Victoria Principal

3. What is the one thing that all Springer's guests are missing?
   a. prime-time exposure
   b. SAG pay scale
   c. a good director
   d. chromosomes

4. You can prove that all men are not created equal by just looking:
   a. where they grew up
   b. at their accomplishments
   c. at their parents
   d. in a locker room

5. The smartest move for a husband who has just insulted his wife is to:
   a. give her a dozen roses
   b. apologize immediately
   c. take her out for a romantic dinner
   d. disappear from the face of the earth

6. After spending a weekend in bed watching those tearjerker movies, a woman may gain:
   a. inner peace
   b. a sense of relief
   c. a better grip on her problems
   d. eight pounds

7. One of the world's most celebrated punches was given by:
   a. Muhammad Ali
   b. Joe Frazier
   c. Mike Tyson
   d. Zsa Zsa Gabor

The answers to all of the above are d, as in "down for the count."

Scoring:

1–3 correct: Sucker punch.

4–7 correct: A TKO.

FOUR

Women's Luncheons: Pass the Prozac, Please

One of the basic rights guaranteed to women under the Constitution is the right to do lunch. We gals take this seriously. Women have elevated lunch from a mundane experience into an art form. For us, a justifiable cause for lunch is any occasion imaginable, from celebration to crisis. Celebratory lunches are for events like:

Birthdays
Engagements
Baby showers
Face-lifts
Divorce—in many cases

Support lunches are to help women going through any of the following crises:

Boredom
Marital spats
Bladder infections
Unplanned pregnancies
Divorce—in some cases

Let me categorically state from the beginning that the one thing we do not actually do at lunch is eat. We do everything but. Why? Because our group luncheons have mutated into epic productions, like a major Broadway show. We have specific agendas that must be completed during lunch. The problem is that by the time we get through these rituals, there's hardly any time to eat.

Here's a typical agenda we follow during one of our luncheons:

12 NOON

Great Expectations

Most of the time we won't order until everyone is present and accounted for. This means one thing only: group starvation. The women have more excuses for being late than a pregnant teenager. Here are just a few of the kinds of emergencies that keep the gals from being on time:

* Emergency trips to high school to pick up daughter ailing with cramps and menorrhea[1]
* Trip to the ER for broken acrylic nail
* Husband appears home unexpectedly—emergency nooner requested[2]
* Nanny failed to show—emergency trip to drugstore for Valium

It usually takes anywhere from fifteen minutes to an hour for the latecomers to get there. During this period, there is a minimum of seventy-seven cell phone calls from absentees reporting their exact locations on the freeways and estimating their ETAs.

1 P.M.

Robert's Rules of Ordering

After everyone arrives, the gabbing and gossiping erupts into full swing. Everyone is catching up, because we haven't seen each

---

1. AKA: not being prepared for the test.
2. Technically, a mercy mission.

other for ages—three to four days. The waiter comes by to take our orders, but we keep sending him away. Nobody has even opened a menu, much less decided on what to order. By the third trip to our table, he is totally pissed but manages his best customer smile. But, as they say, he ain't seen nothin' yet. The guy has no clue what he's in for when we actually get around to ordering. Not one of us would actually order off the menu if it killed us.

There are dieters, vegans, lactose intolerant, and the highly allergic all represented in our group. All have their special requests and proceed to make a bazillion substitutions. By the time we're through, the original dishes we ordered are completely unidentifiable.

Western Omelet—no egg yolks, peppers, onions, cheese, or broccoli. No toast. Substitute whole-wheat bagel with lite cream cheese.

Chicken Caesar Salad—No chicken. Substitute grilled shrimp. Shaved Parmesan only. Balsamic vinaigrette on the side. No dark romaine. Only organic baby Bibb lettuce is acceptable.

Cheeseburger and Fries—No bun. No cheese. No fries. No meat. Veggie burger only. Cottage cheese and fresh fruit substituted for the fries.

Cobb Salad—Hold the bacon, eggs, cheese, ham, and dressing. Everything else supplied by a Jenny Craig foil pouch.

By now, the waiter is sweating profusely as he writes a volume rivaling *War and Peace*. From his expression, he is close to wielding a steak knife. More bad news. Just wait until the women start sending everything back. He's going to be in therapy the rest of the month. Scratch that. For the rest of his life.

2:30 P.M.

Get the Picture?

Women operate under the principle that we must record all our activities on celluloid for posterity. But the photos can't be just any unposed shots of us acting normally. No way, José. They have to be epic group shots, staged with more attention to detail than a *Vogue* photo shoot.

First we get up from our seats and stand in a group pose. Then somebody decides that the lighting and background are all wrong. So we move to another spot. Then somebody complains that the taller gals need to stand in the back, or there are too many blondes grouped together—yada-yada-yada. Everybody thinks she's a director.

So we futz around for another fifteen minutes to get the perfect shot. Did somebody say anal-retentive? Obsessive-compulsive? Women with too much time on their hands? No? Well, if the Nike[3] fits, wear it. In order not to leave anybody out, we need somebody else to take the picture. That's when we snag our waiter, who by now is instinctively avoiding us like anthrax. But we insist. Just as he's about to click, somebody says, "Wait. I forgot to put lipstick on." So we try again. Click. We hear, "Oh, no. Can you take that over? I closed my eyes." After the eighth shot, we finally get it right. To say the waiter is anxious to get out of there is the understatement of the year. The guy takes off so fast, he leaves skid marks.

Just when you think it's safe to sit down again—not so fast. The photo op is far from over. Now the girls want to pose in smaller groups of two and three, in various spots around the room. At this point, we have made such a spectacle of ourselves, the other diners are close to mutiny.

3 P.M.

Grease Your Palms

At last our food arrives. Thank God, it's chow time. Hold it— there's one more item on our agenda. We have to decide on the best day for our next luncheon. This is when we drag out our Palm Pilots and go over our schedules by the week, then the month. There is a law of physics that states when more than eight women

3. Or Nikon.

are planning an event on the same day, the odds of it ever occurring are 1,000,000,000 to 1.

This is how this dialogue goes:

> How about Tuesday, the third?
> No. Karen and Diane can't make it. They have yoga class.
> Okay. Thursday, the fifth?
> Nope. Wendy and Nancy are out of town.
> Okay—everyone scroll to the next week. How about Monday the ninth?
> Uh-uh. Jan and Gail have their alien abduction group meeting.

So between the nail appointments, school meetings, and doctor and dentist appointments, it's a no go. As usual, we come to the conclusion that there will never be a date when every single gal can make it. Then we're faced with the unpleasant task of picking a date somebody has to miss. Meanwhile our lunches have gotten colder than the Robert Blake murder trail.

3:30 P.M.

Sale of the Century

I have never been to lunch with women where somebody wasn't selling something. When six or more women gather for lunch with their checkbooks, it is the perfect venue for hawking—anything. Some of the women design and sell their own jewelry. Others bring ceramic pieces. Then there are always the countless items offered from charities. The samples and catalogs are passed around, oohed and aahed over. This takes precedence over any other unimportant activity, like eating.

The table is inundated with merchandise, and everyone begins filling out order forms. There are cosmetic articles, flower pens in hand-painted pots for fundraising events, Girl Scout cookies, and beaded purses. Wait a minute. This isn't lunch—it's a swap meet.

CELL PHONES
Ladies, Charge Your Batteries

Contributing to this carnival atmosphere, add the sound of eight cell phones ringing nonstop. Calls are coming in from every corner of the world, calls of global importance from:

Kids—who forgot their lunches[4] and have fainted from sugar withdrawal

Salons—reminding gals of 4 P.M. bikini waxes

Girlfriends—who got dumped by their latest boyfriend and are suicidal

Lawyers—the family shih tzu bit the groomer, and she's filing a lawsuit

4 P.M.
Let Me Outta Here

While all this stuff is going on, nobody has taken one bite of food. Somebody remarks about the time and all the women jump up, because they're late for carpooling. Once again, the waiter gets barraged. This time he is asked to box up all the uneaten dishes. Time to split the bill. This is a mega-nightmare. Do we ever just divide it up eight ways? Nooooo. That would be too simple. Even the CPAs at Arthur Andersen would take early retirement rather than have to figure out this fiasco. All the women start shouting over one another.

"I had a Cobb salad and one glass of wine." "I had the appetizer only with a cappuccino." "Wait a sec—you have to add the three desserts for Becky, Sandy, and Diedre." "No—that's wrong. Two of us had the shrimp pesto with the crab appetizer. Wendy had the pesto with no appetizer."

Oy vey! At this point I plop down a twenty-dollar bill, gulp down an Advil, and get the hell out of there. I must get home and listen to my meditation tapes while breathing into a paper bag. It will take the rest of the afternoon for me to calm down from this relaxing lunch. I need the time to recharge my batteries.[5]

---

4. Three Kit Kat bars.
5. On my cell phone and Palm Pilot.

Pass the Prozac, Please

1. If your ladies' lunch is getting too disruptive, the waiter might ask you to move to:
   a. a different table
   b. the back room
   c. the bar area
   d. another restaurant

2. The best tip to give your waiter at a group luncheon is:
   a. 15 percent
   b. 20 percent
   c. 25 percent
   d. "don't wait on this table"

3. The most popular item ordered for a woman's fortieth birthday luncheon is:
   a. a giant balloon bouquet
   b. a double chocolate fudge cake
   c. three dozen roses
   d. a male stripper

4. What is the most dreaded phrase a waiter can hear from a large group of women:
   a. "the party is canceled"
   b. "we need another table"
   c. "the service was terrible"
   d. "separate checks, please"

5. The most appropriate gift to give a woman who has been through a bad divorce is:
    a. a support luncheon
    b. *The Prophet* by Kahlil Gibran
    c. a complimentary spa day
    d. a leather studded thong

6. Before going out to a women's luncheon, don't forget:
    a. to check the date
    b. your gift for the honoree
    c. your credit card
    d. to eat

7. A bachelorette luncheon should never be given without:
    a. champagne
    b. table favors
    c. live music
    d. a designated driver

The answers to all of the above are d, as in "dressing on the side."

Scoring:

1–3 correct: Take a table.

4–7 correct: Take a Tagamet.

FIVE

*M*en:
A Testament
to Testosterone

Okay. Whaddya say? I think it's about time for a little male bash-ing. Aw, come on. Don't go getting all uptight on me. There's at least a bazillion things guys do that drive us nuts. You know the stuff I'm talking about. Those annoying behaviors like being . . . present. Let's face it. In the world of women, there isn't a topic that's been discussed, debated, and analyzed more than how men behave.[1] It's been the subject of novels, movies, and eight-hour therapy sessions. We spend a good deal of our lives[2] trying to figure men out.

Well, I've got a news flash. It's not all that hard. There's a basic premise that I have figured out. Two forces drive men's behavior: ego and testosterone. I call it the E.T. factor. Here's the logic: If men = E.T. and E.T. = aliens, then men = aliens. Yes, that's right. All men are aliens. Once you embrace this basic tenet, the rest is simple. Here are some of the E.T.-driven behaviors most promi-nent in men:

1. Correction—misbehave.
2. And our money.

CATEGORY ONE

THE THINGS YOU DO

Denial—Who ever said denial was a problem unique to women? Wrong. Compared to us, men absolutely live in the state of denial.[3] They have since time began. Even the great thinker Aristotle publicly spoke about men taking responsibility in one of his most famous oratories: "If it ain't real, you don't have to deal." Oooops. Sorry. That was Johnnie Cochran.

Weighty Issues—We gals aren't the only ones who tend to spread out during middle age. Men also start taking up a lot more square footage after forty. But their egos won't allow them to admit it to anybody, especially themselves. When my husband can't zip up his jeans, he immediately reaches one of the following conclusions:

1. The cleaner shrunk the denim
2. Levi Strauss is cutting them smaller
3. The store put the wrong waist size on them
4. He's too "sophisticated"[4] to wear jeans anyway

Hypochondria—Most men refuse to see a doctor. I think it's because they basically don't want a doctor telling them what's wrong with them. Once again, it's the E.T. factor kicking in. Men don't want to hear some Harvard Medical School hotshot half his age telling him he's in lousy shape. Especially when the doctor says he must lose twenty pounds and lower his cholesterol by giving up his healthy diet of beer and Cheez Doodles.

This is how we wives and girlfriends ended up with the job of diagnosing them. If you ask me, I think that all men over fifty should be married to nurses. I can tell you that in my house, not a day goes by that I don't get a "medical report" from my husband.

---

3. Lifelong residents.
4. Translation: porky.

He feels compelled to tell me about each and every symptom—real or imaginary. Every night before going to bed, he performs a thorough "body check." This is one of our typical conversations that take place after his nightly ritual:

"Hey, honey. Would you look at this, please?"

"Look at what?"

"This . . . this big lump here."

"Lump? I don't see anything."

"Yes, you do. *This* . . . right here."

"Oh. You mean that little pimple? That's an ingrown hair."

"No, I don't think so. It's a lump. I think it might be cancer."

"Trust me. I've never heard of a cancerous hair."

And so, inch by square inch it goes on, until he finally finds something that he thinks will stump me.

"Honey, have a look at this. Now, *this* is serious. A black mole has suddenly come up on my chest—right below my nipple. Do you think I need to have it removed?"

"I think you need to remove that leaky fountain pen from your shirt pocket."

Damn, I'm good!

Just when I think I have calmed him down, and he's finally symptom free, there's more bad news ahead in the world of hypochondria. HBO has just announced they're showing a remake of *Brian's Song*. God help us all. Every woman on the planet knows that back in the '70s, the original *Brian's Song* was responsible for a mass epidemic of hypochondria that affected all American males. It put more fear in men than the shower scene from *Psycho* ever did to women. Every guy who watched it was convinced he was dying of terminal cancer. Oh brother! Somebody renew my medical license. After he watches it, I'm going to be on call for another five years.

Emotional Problems—Men never admit to having them. They feel they are strictly female dysfunctions. But the thing is, they don't want us to have them either. If I complain to my husband that I'm bored with life, unfulfilled, and depressed, it sends him into a mental tailspin. All he wants is for me and my problems to disappear. This is how the male mind processes a problem and resolves it (approximately six seconds):

First thought: "Man, oh, man. Her whining is driving me nuts."

Second thought: "She thinks we need counseling. Should I go just to shut her up?"

Third thought: "Should I agree to go to our minister with her, just to get a few days of peace?"

Fourth thought: "Or would it be better to sit down with her and discuss her feelings?"

Fifth thought: "Am I part of the problem?"

Sixth thought: "Naaaahhhhh. The best thing to do is ignore it, and it will go away."

CATEGORY TWO
NEATNESS COUNTS

Okay, so shoot me. I know that I'm going off like a shoe bomb here. I could fill the rest of the book with negative observations about men—which isn't necessarily a bad thing. But in my list of the top five, this one is universally true. All guys are slobs. Even if his mother were Emily Post, it wouldn't matter. When it comes to picking up after himself, a man is incapable of grasping this concept. Again, it's an E.T. thing. The male ego tells him that anything to do with tidying up is women's work. No kidding. It's a real phobia. He is afraid if he hangs up his own clothes or does his own laundry, he will instantly turn gay.

Trust me. You can't fight it. Just plan on pulling double-duty in this department for the rest of your life. Here are some of the areas that men avoid more than lengthy foreplay:

* After getting dressed and grooming themselves, most men leave for work looking like the epitome of neatness. But they also leave something else—a massive wake of chaos behind. Why is it that my husband can slam dunk a basketball through a twelve-inch hoop from ten feet away, but he can't manage to drop his dirty clothes into a hamper with a three-foot rim?

* Ditto for the bathroom. Who would think that this well-groomed guy in his three-piece suit and impeccably groomed hair would leave dribble stains all around the bottom of the toilet bowl? And would he ever think to mop them up? Not in this lifetime, Mr. Clean. And there's no way I know of that I'm ever going to correct this, either. What will it take to get him to aim straight? Do I have to paint a bull's-eye in the bowl?

* To a man, the concept of a clothes hanger is as alien as a curling iron.[5] When my husband undresses after work, each piece of clothing is left in a different location—on the floor. If I ask him to hang everything up, he always says the same thing: "Just leave them there. If I decide to get dressed again, I'll know where they are."

* This scholarly dissertation wouldn't be complete without at least a mention of the hair-in-the-drain thing. I have learned from firsthand experience that I'm at great risk if I shower directly after my husband. I cannot just get into the shower and turn the water on full blast. If I did, the water would be up to my nostrils in two minutes.

Here's the thing. My husband has a full head of hair, plus a beard. He should keep Roto-Rooter on speed dial. However, the fact

5. Can't tell one from another.

is that he wouldn't clean his hair out of the drain if his life depended on it. So, for his own safety, I insist he wear a flotation device.

CATEGORY THREE

CAN I BE OF ASSISTANCE?

Asking for Help—A big part of the E.T. syndrome is that men feel they need to know *everything*. To them, it's a sign of total weakness to ever, God forbid, ask for help. The three areas they have made famous are:

* *Asking for directions:* We gals are all too familiar with this one. I'll share a typical scenario that every American woman repeatedly endures. Our friends who live in the next town invite us for dinner. I say to my husband, "Do I need to get directions?" He invariably says, "Naaah. I know where the Smiths live." So we leave at 7 P.M. in plenty of time for the 7:30 dinner. Within five minutes, he takes the wrong exit.[6] Then he circles back twice, each time ending up on a different interstate. Soon we're on a rural two-lane highway, passing cows and reading signs written in a foreign language.

    After an hour, I cautiously ask him if he's lost. Naturally, he's furious. He loses it and starts yelling he knows exactly where he is.[7] But I know better. He doesn't have a clue where he is. He doesn't even know what state he's in. But I do. He's in the state of confusion.

* *Won't read instructions:* What's up with guys and instruction books? Trying to get them to read one is worse than trying to make them write a thank-you note. All I know is this. My house looks like a Circuit City warehouse.

6. From the on-ramp.
7. Behind the wheel, for sure.

We have boxes of unused DVD players, VCRs, cell phones, and a Tivo. All because my husband won't take the time to read the instruction books. You would think they were written in Japanese.[8]

He says programming the VCR takes a Ph.D. He needs an M.A. to get through the DVD booklet. He should have at least a 150 IQ to figure out what the Tivo instruction manual says. Good grief. We're drowning in high-tech alphabet soup. And guess what? All the letters are E. and T.

✸ *Won't hire a professional:* Men have to feel like "manly men" all the time. It's an Irish Spring thing. They think it's a weakness to admit they have no clue how to fix things, like a leaky faucet or an electrical outlet. So they put on this bravura performance, trying to prove they can do all these masculine tasks. And what's the best way to go about it? Would they ever consider reading a do-it-your-self book or watching a step-by-step video? No sirree Bob . . . Vila. They're going to wing it.

My husband's plumbing and electrical repairs gave us memorable results: a flood and electrical fire in our home. So listen to me. It's safer and cheaper to stage an intervention. Gather your caring and concerned family members together and have them break the news to your husband that he is mechanically impaired. It's called tough love. But it's worth it. In the long run, it will save your marriage, your home, and about $5,000 in repairs.

8. They are.

A Testament to Testosterone

1. A man is happiest with a woman who is:
   a. uncomplaining
   b. loving
   c. sexy
   d. inflatable

2. Which decorated soldier is a role model for most men?
   a. General Patton
   b. Admiral Halsey
   c. Colonel Potter
   d. Sergeant Bilko

3. Men leave all major decisions to their:
   a. wives
   b. bosses
   c. accountants
   d. penises

4. A man's greatest medical fear is having a:
   a. stroke
   b. heart attack
   c. brain tumor
   d. prostate exam

5. Most men will try to fill an emotional hole with:
   a. the love of a woman
   b. a good therapist
   c. Bible study
   d. liquor and Velveeta

6. Men identify with male culinary figures on TV. The show they love to watch is *Cooking with* . . . :
   a. Emeril LaGasse
   b. Wolfgang Puck
   c. Justin Wilson
   d. Hannibal Lecter

7. Which gray-haired statesman is admired by men of all ages?
   a. Aristotle
   b. Judge Antonin Scalia
   c. Senator Strom Thurmond
   d. Gary Condit

The answers to all of the above are d, as in "detour."

Scoring:

1–3 correct: You're in the ballpark.
4–7 correct: You're in Jurassic Park.

SIX

Singles Bars: Who Let the Dogs Out?

I'm always kidding my husband that he's never going to get rid of me. I'll never divorce him. No matter what. He can ignore me, yell at me, forget all my birthdays, and force me to watch six hours of back-to-back Jean-Claude Van Damme movies. But that's still not grounds for divorce.[1] Sure, I love him. But you want to know the real truth? Okay—brace yourself. If I were single again, I'd shoot myself.

I know lots of single women, and believe me, it takes too much time and energy to live this lifestyle. It's a ton of work. Single women spend all their time dolling up, dancing, and staying out late, in hot pursuit of an eligible man. Give me a break. You need more stamina than a contestant on *Survivor*.

Single women report that it's slim pickin's out there. Many of the good ones are taken. From what I can tell, they're right. To me, middle-aged dating is like going to the supermarket at 3 A.M. All the goods have been opened or tampered with.

First you've got to wade through the dating pool, then reel in

1. The Van Damme marathon comes pretty close.

a suitable guy to go out with. After you find him, it can take months or years to develop a relationship. The number one thing in a relationship everybody is looking for is honesty. So when you learn to fake that, you're in good shape. But if you break up, it takes months to get back into circulation. The whole process can go on longer than a Merchant Ivory film.

Did you hear about the new practice of speed dating? I think it's a great idea. Here's how it works: A group of men and women meet at a designated location, like a restaurant. They pair off in couples, with three minutes allotted for an interview. In that short time, most of the couples can tell if there is some chemistry or not. Then a bell rings, and they're on to the next person. In this format, a gal can effectively interview about twenty men in one session. Then she can go back to a guy who was of particular interest for a second look.

Great idea! It's kind of a "one-minute manager" concept. And it sure works better here than in the bedroom. Let's face it. It doesn't take a woman more than three seconds to decide if the guy is a dork. If not, she gets her chance to find out if he's somebody she wants to know better. If I were single, this is how I would want to screen men for dating. I like the fast track. After fifty, everything we do only lasts a few minutes, anyway.

BARROOM BINGO

I think that nowadays, the avenues[2] open to women for meeting men are just abysmal. There are those horrendous singles bars where the men act like they're at a cattle auction. So who are these guys anyway? They aren't exactly in your prime-rib class, themselves.[3] For starters, most of them drink too much. I don't know about you, but I want a man who can raise the bar, not close it.

2. More like back alleys.
3. Rump roasts.

Then there are those god-awful karaoke bars. They mix two things together that should never meet: people who shouldn't drink and people who shouldn't sing.

But single women are hell-bent on a mission. They've invested a lot of effort learning the secrets of successfully attracting men. However, in these bars, they're competing with a hundred other women just like themselves—only ten years younger. This isn't an easy task. The competition is stiff.[4] So, in order to "work the room" successfully, you have to become a pro in the following areas:

Singles Olympic Events

Hair Tossing and Fluffing—The technique of hair tossing must be executed with practiced skill or a woman could suffer major whiplash. First, it requires really long hair with big volume. Then as she flirts, it seductively falls over her face at five-second intervals. Then with the synchronized movement of a trained gymnast, she flips her head sharply, swooshing her hair into glamorous waves around her face. This can take years of practice, but it's incredibly effective. Guys are total suckers for it.

The fluffing part requires a woman to have those seven-inch acrylic nails, which she runs through her hair. Pump up that volume, baybee. For optimum results, a woman should do this while wearing a clingy sleeveless top that shows off her toned biceps and reveals the graceful bulge of her silicone breasts.

Leg Crossing—Time flies when you're in hot pursuit. Just remember, you've only got a few hours to show off all the goods. So use that miniskirt to its best advantage. Barstool sitting is an art unto itself. A gal should perch herself in full view and then seductively cross her legs. Just a tease, though. You have to be careful not to show the whole enchilada.

---

4. Not as stiff as the guys at the bar.

When done properly, a woman can have a guy groveling at her feet.[5] Men are putty in the presence of gorgeous gams. I think the ultimate role model for leg crossing is Sharon Stone. Who could forget her classic leg-crossing scene in *Basic Instinct*? With the cool fluid movement of sinew over sinew, she managed to put every man in the country in heat. Talk about your hot-blooded American males. They nearly cooked themselves.

Cleavage Flexing—There is a minimum requirement for this event: a 36C bust. And if you don't have it, don't bother going to a singles bar. The total number of cubic feet of silicone at a singles bar is staggering. Plus, it's all encased in clingy spandex tops. Even if the women aren't wearing off-the-shoulder styles, they eventually get there.

Décolletage is key in this event. It allows women to make practiced moves, showing off their assets to their best advantage. Through precisely executed movements like flexing, shoulder shrugging, and leaning at a 45-degree angle, they make their bosoms appear larger than they really are.[6] Any one of these moves will have men eating out of their hand.[7]

Eyelash Batting—After all the posturing is complete, the next step is to pick out a hottie and make eye contact with him. This can be a really tough proposition because most guys have that blank stare—like your dog gets when you put him on the phone. The women who are most effective at this never leave the house without wearing at least three coats of Maybelline ultra-lengthening, ultra-thickening, ultra-volumizing mascara. After spotting her mark, she begins batting those lids faster than a hummingbird's wings.

Her eyes dart to his, make contact, then she coquettishly flutters them and looks away. Make no mistake. This is a time-proven technique women have employed for eons. This move is the perfect

5. And looking up her skirt.
6. A rearview mirror works, too.
7. Kibbles and Bits.

vehicle for getting what she wants. And the men are only too happy to go along for the ride. When eyelash batting is accompanied by cleavage flexing and strategic bun positioning, a guy is dead meat.

After the guy is reeled in and begins a conversation with a girl, Phase II begins:

Singles Bar Banter

After they get together, it's time for the couple to prove how incredibly hot each of them is. This is where the famous "pickup" lines come into play. The truth is that these lines are lamer than the guy in *Dude, Where's My Car?* But it's a necessary part of the game playing. It can even get a little dangerous—you might die of boredom.

Scenario #1—A guy comes over to two gals at the bar. Both women are beautiful. One is an olive-skinned Latin beauty. The other is a blond who is so pale, she is nearly transparent.

Guy Pickup Line: "Wow! You girls are really gorgeous. You must be sisters."

Scenario #2— A guy approaches a sexy gal wearing skin-tight spandex pants and a low-cut clingy jersey top. He shamelessly ogles her buns and says, "How do you get into those pants?"

Gal Pickup Line: "You can start by buying me a drink."

Often, after the first twenty seconds, it's apparent the guy has the personality of a dial tone. When you're losing interest faster than a Keating Savings and Loan, it's time to dump him fast. Any of the following lines will get the job done:

Exit Lines

* Don't you have a cousin you should be dating?
* I have a two-week-old baby—from a previous marriage.
* I'm running low on estrogen—and I have a gun.
* I'm in a bigger state of sexual confusion than Sinéad O'Connor.

✳ I'm bi . . . polar.

✳ I think you are missing something. Like . . . a chromosome.

✳ Is your career goal targeting your lats?

✳ I see you're one of the Rogaine failure cases.

✳ If teeth were brains, you'd rule the planet.

Pretty neat, huh? Oh, you don't have to tell me. Just call me a helpless romantic.

Who Let the Dogs Out?

1. Your marriage is on the rocks when your wife:
    a. seeks counseling
    b. suffers depression
    c. talks rudely to you
    d. starts dating

2. The leading cause of the increase in Porsche 911 sales is:
    a. a healthy economy
    b. their top-notch advertising
    c. bigger per capita income
    d. baldness

3. The difference between a dog and a fox is:
    a. different species
    b. domesticated vs. feral
    c. blood types
    d. about five drinks

4. A woman's favorite position is:
    a. the missionary
    b. on top
    c. #5 in the Kama Sutra
    d. CEO

5. Getting a lot of sex is necessary to men of all ages because:
    a. it's a biological need
    b. it's emotionally comforting
    c. it's an ego thing
    d. they need stories to tell their friends

6. The only mechanical device that turns women on is:
    a. a vibrator
    b. a naughty video
    c. a vibrating bed
    d. a Mercedes Benz 380 SL

7. When a man talks to a woman in a bar, he always pictures her:
    a. at his apartment
    b. kissing him
    c. as a perfect wife
    d. butt-naked

The answers to all of the above are d, as in "dog day afternoon."

Scoring:

1–3 correct: You found yourself a mogul.

4–7 correct: You picked a mongrel.

SEVEN

Beauty Salons: From Hair to Eternity

To the casual observer, a beauty salon is a place where you get your hair done and maybe indulge in a little gossip. Wrong. At least not the beauty salon I go to. Mine is much, much more. It's actually a front for a multilevel consortium offering a vast array of goods and services. Getting your hair done is merely an appetizer on their menu.

On any given day, it's like Circus Vargas. Every chair in the place is occupied with women getting clipped, curled, blow-dried, dyed, or shampooed. There's even an area where a cosmetician does makeovers. My salon also employs several manicurists, who book separately for manicures and pedicures. Straight across from the front door is a jewelry kiosk where a woman sells original designs she makes from lovely crystal beads. And at any given moment, there is a steady stream of vendors passing though, hawking T-shirts, paintings, potted plants, and even fresh produce. Get the picture? This is no beauty parlor. It's a flea market.

However, there is something going on that is much more fascinating than sales. It's the interaction of the clients and their hairdressers. There is no bond on earth like this one. No matter how private a person you are, once you sit in that chair, you feel compelled to spill your guts. Your hairdresser becomes your shrink, psychic adviser, doctor, and legal counselor. There is no topic imaginable that's too personal or beyond their scope of knowledge. These women are omniscient. They make Miss Cleo look like an amateur.[1]

Between my shampoo, cut, and blow-dry, I have plenty of time to vent about or overhear topics like these:

1. Della's husband's latest affair
2. What a monster my mother-in-law is
3. Beth's teenager's drug and alcohol problems
4. My raging yeast infection
5. Cindy's suspicions that her fifteen-year-old is having sex with her boyfriend

Trust me. Whatever problems I have, my beautician has first-hand knowledge of them, too. She is not only a good listener, but she is the one person who is always there for me,[2] to offer her expertise. However, I try not to get carried away. When I am confiding my innermost secrets to her, the entire salon is my audience. Everybody in the place seems to possess super hearing skills.

No matter how softly I speak, what I say *will* be heard, remembered, and repeated for the next six months by at least twenty women. What's up with that? How are these women able to hear every word I'm saying, even if I'm whispering? Half of them are sitting there with cotton wrapped around their ears. They couldn't all be lip-readers—could they?

Not on your Beltones, baybee. Here's my personal theory, which has recently been endorsed by the greatest minds in science.[3] Think about this factoid. Many of the women are listening while getting a "weave." This is a process during which the hairdresser

1. Having a bad-hair day.
2. By appointment.
3. Mr. Wizard and the late Carl Sagan.

separates the hair into tiny sections, paints them with bleach, then wraps them up in a sheath of aluminum foil. So each of these women has, like, a hundred tinfoil antennas sticking out of her head. And with this kind of receiving equipment, they could pick up Radio Free Europe.

This is not necessarily a bad thing. The biggest advantage is that no matter what I'm complaining about, every woman listening to me has experienced the same problems. At least twice. So they feel very comfortable about jumping into my private conversation and dispensing advice. Women are not shy about informing me that:

1. I'm handling my problem all wrong.
2. I'm clueless about what's really going on.
3. I'm an idiot.

But they mean it in a good way. So I just sit tight. Besides all the free advice, I also get referrals of names of the best professionals in town, their addresses, and their direct phone lines.

Let's eavesdrop on some typical conversations on any given day:

SEXUAL DYSFUNCTION THERAPY

Kathy B. in Chair #1: "I'm having a terrible time with my husband. We're constantly fighting. He claims I'm never in the mood for sex anymore. The last time we did it was six months ago. So what's his point? At least he's getting something. I'm going through menopause, and I'm tired and anxious all the time. My doctor told me to take Paxil. I'm more relaxed now, but I have no sex drive. Charlie keeps threatening to have an affair."

Ursula G. in Chair #5: "Oh honey, you don't have to tell me about it! I went through the same thing last year with Eddie. It was awful. He actually started going online to those porno chat rooms. He'd be up all night improving his typing skills—with one hand, if you catch my drift."

Sally R. in Chair #4: "Yeah, like the Gulf Stream."

Ursula G: in Chair #5: "But then I found the greatest gyno in the world. Dr. Ann Claymore at Scripps Clinic. She prescribed small doses of the male hormone testosterone. It did wonders to perk up our sex life. And by the way, Eddie gave up typing."

DRUG AND ALCOHOL COUNSELING

Judy C. in Chair #8: "Bobby, my sixteen-year-old, has been coming home drunk from parties. I've read him the riot act at least a dozen times. I even grounded him for a month. But I am terrified that it's going to become a habitual problem with him. I don't know what to do next, short of giving him a Breathalyzer test every time he comes home from a party."

Patty R. in Chair #7: "Sweetie, you need to talk to Nancy, sitting over there in Carolyn's chair. After struggling with her son's alcohol problems for a year, she put him in that Promises rehab place. It cost her a small fortune, but he's doing great. He met a lot of actors there, and they helped him get some acting jobs. Now he's got a whole new career. You can see him in a bit part on *NYPD Blue* next week."

Nancy J. in Chair #2: "It's true. Darren is doing really well now. He's been clean and sober for over a year. After struggling with his own alcohol problems, he's totally committed to helping other young people overcome their addictions. Call him. Darren will be eager to share his own experiences with Bobby. You can reach him through his agent at 555-8876, leave a voice mail, or e-mail him at darrenmegastar@hotmail.com."

DIAGNOSTIC CENTER FOR DEADLY DISEASES

Wendy G. in the Makeup Chair: "I've been feeling completely exhausted for months now. I can hardly get myself out of bed and get dressed in the morning. I've seen three specialists, an acupuncturist, and an herbalist. But I still feel awful. After having dozens of tests, none of the doctors know what's wrong with me."

Darcy V. in the Manicure Chair: "Darling, I do. You've got that virus Cher had—it's called ummm—some person's name—oh, yeah—Epstein-Barr. I know, because my neighbor's elderly mother, Ida Rosenberg, was diagnosed with it not long ago. She suffered all the same symptoms you did. But luckily, her wonderful internist, Dr. Harold Ibsen, diagnosed it and treated her. Call him and tell him I referred you."

Wendy G.: "Thank you. It's such a comfort to know there's help. So how is Ida feeling?"

Darcy V.: "Well, as a matter of fact, she died about two weeks ago. But they think it was from something else. Not to worry. Just give Dr. Ibsen a call."

CIRCUITOUS CONNECTIONS

Betsy Y. in Chair #6: "I'm so frustrated I can't stand it. For the past eight weeks, I've been trying to get tickets for *The Lion King.* Every time I call the box office either it's either busy, or they say they're sold out. I promised my ten-year-old daughter I'd take her and she's heartbroken."

Terry M. in Chair #7: "Did you call the 5646 box office number? You did? Well, that's your problem. You'll never get anywhere that way. This is how you do it. My brother knows this girl who works for *The Lion King*'s head choreographer's assistant. Call 555-6667 and ask for Sheherazade. Tell her you're a personal friend of Tony Habib's sister and you want two tickets for Saturday night. I guarantee you'll get them. Oh, yeah—she adds on an extra 30 percent for her handling fee."

Marilyn T. in Chair #10: "I can't believe what I'm hearing. She's better off dealing with a scalper."

Okay. So much for the therapy sessions. On to the good stuff—the essence of the salon experience. A body perm? A henna rinse? Naaaah. The gossip. If I want to find out anything about what's happening in town, on TV, in Hollywood, or in any third world country, I ask my beautician.

While I'm in the chair I can get the dirt on anybody I know—or would like to know. I can find out who's cheating on whom, who's dating whom, who's sleeping with whom, and who's in rehab. I ask you—who needs the FBI? In this business, the beauticians have a file on everybody.

When I finish getting my hair done, I sometimes still crave a little more gossiping time. No problem. Here are just a few of the services offered to extend my stay:[4]

manicure	hot oil treatments	leg waxing
pedicure	cuticle treatment	electrolysis
facial	body perm	facials
bikini wax	cold wave perm	herbal wrap
hair extensions	massage	aromatherapy
eyebrow waxing	eyelash dyeing	tanning cream
acrylic nails	wig styling	application

Amazing, isn't it? The services are becoming so sophisticated, it's just a matter of time until they'll be performing face-lifts in the waxing rooms. These hairdressers can do anything. Who knows what's next? My money's on cloning.

4. For the rest of the week.

From Hair to Eternity

1. To make a bikini wax less painful, you should:
    a. keep your knees bent
    b. heat the wax to 103 degrees
    c. apply talcum powder first
    d. remain unconscious

2. The sharpest instruments in a beauty salon are:
    a. cutting shears
    b. toenail clippers
    c. trimming razors
    d. the women's tongues

3. What does every beautician wear underneath her smock?
    a. a support bra
    b. deodorant shields
    c. a comfortable shirt
    d. a wire

4. Most clients spend approximately $100 a week on:
    a. hair weaving
    b. makeup and hair products
    c. electrolysis
    d. hush money

5. What kind of tip should you give the shampoo girl:
    a. $5.00
    b. 15 percent of your total bill
    c. not more than $2.00
    d. "keep your mouth shut"

6. After having two-inch acrylic nails applied, a woman is considered:
    a. well groomed and polished
    b. wealthy and extravagant
    c. glamorous and sophisticated
    d. armed and dangerous

7. A potential chemical hazard that might occur at a beauty salon is:
    a. toxic fume inhalation
    b. caustic chemical burns
    c. chemical spill
    d. silicone spill

The answers to all of the above are d, as in "dye job."

Scoring:

1–3 correct: Get a new hairdo.

4–7 correct: Get a new identity.

EIGHT

$\mathcal{P}$arenting: Homeland Security

As a biologist, I subscribe to Darwin's theory of the survival of the fittest. It makes perfect sense to me. Based on this principle, I am going to make this prediction: The human race is destined for extinction. How come? Because today's parents are raising a generation of wusses.

Aw, don't go getting your Diaper Genies in an uproar. Look at it this way. Years ago, when my parents were kids, nobody was raised in the lap of luxury. In fact, there weren't any laps, because everybody was standing in a breadline. My parents grew up in a time when every day was a struggle just to stay alive. They had to cope with incredible adversities like the Great Depression, inadequate health care, and no Internet. Then along came Prohibition. Geez Louise. No wonder everyone was depressed. My generation, the Boomers, had it better, but it was still no picnic. We had to face the threat of nuclear war, polio epidemics, and Mamie Eisenhower.

My own children were fortunate enough to grow up with the benefits of modern technology, better health care, and the determination to make the world a safer place. But, when I look around me today, I think these good intentions have, somehow, become a compulsion. Today's parents are totally obsessed with protecting their kids from every kind of threat, real or imaginary.

From where I stand, I think kids are being raised like a generation of weaklings. Sure, we all agree that safety is a good thing. But too much of a good thing can backfire. The Yuppie parents of today are practically raising their kids in a bubble. It's no wonder we developed the technology to clone human beings. We had to. Nobody's going to be fit enough to survive, unless he has a bunch of clones for backup.

What happened to those good old, devil-may-care days? When I was a kid growing up in Connecticut, my mom pushed us out the door to play in 20-degree temperatures. We stayed outside all day, with wet mittens, galoshes filled with snow, and our ears frozen to our heads. But today? Forget it. Moms wrap their kids in bubble wrap to go outdoors.[1] I've seen kids wearing a helmet just to open a can of tuna, for God's sake.

Here's an overview of how soft the kids have it today versus how tough we had it yesterday:

CAR TRIPS

Yesterday: My parents were big on Sunday afternoon car trips. My folks always said we all needed to get out and get some fresh air. But invariably, they'd roll up the car windows, light up their Luckys, and puff away. Talk about nausea. By the time we got back home, I was the same Nile green shade as my dad's 1952 Chevy.

My brother, my sister, and I were all crammed into the backseat of the car. We didn't have seat belts, either. But the truth is, we wouldn't have used them. We needed to be unrestrained so we could shove and elbow each other for a better view. We had to be tough and fight for every inch of space we got. None of us wanted

---

1. In 75-degree weather.

to get stuck in the spot where the metal springs poked up through the upholstery.

However, those road trips were very educational. We learned a lot on them. Like when my dad took the corner at 65 mph, we learned these three principles of physics:

gravity
balance
inertia

And remember, there was no such thing as an air bag for body protection. When my dad took that curve, we were thrown against the car door, then we ricocheted back like a slingshot. This was the one and only time we wished our two-hundred-pound grandma was back there with us.

Today: The road trip of today is very different from what it used to be. It's more like a ride through an MRI tube. The kids are strapped in with so many restraints, they look like Hannibal Lecter. They are rendered practically immobile, with zero field of vision. What could they possibly learn in this condition? Anger management? They might as well be in a coma for all the sensory stimulation they'll be getting.

MEDICAL CARE

Yesterday: When I was a little girl, I can remember coming down with the Mongolian Flu.[2] This was the most virulent strain of microbes ever found on earth. It was developed and mass produced behind the Iron Curtain.[3] I suffered with terrible chills and fever, chest congestion, a hacking cough, and a stuffed-up head. It was the epitome of misery. All I wanted was to be left alone and expire quickly without life support.

2. Hong Kong wasn't discovered yet.
3. And cultured in 100 proof vodka.

Enter my mom with her arsenal of cures. First, she rubbed Vicks VapoRub on my chest, sending up a cloud of toxic fumes that reeked of camphor. It was heinous. Then, just as I was about to retch my guts out, she'd insist on taking my temperature. Unfortunately, we didn't have the kid-friendly ear thermometers back then. We got the instrument of death. Yep—the rectal thermometer.

Gee thanks, Mom. In the height of my pain and suffering, just what I needed, an instrument of torture shoved into my colon. Just one look at that thing could bring about a miraculous recovery.

Today: At the first sign of the sniffles, Mom goes into her paramedic mode. She tucks her kid into bed under a heated thermal blanket, fires up the hot steam vaporizer, plugs in the air purifier, and wipes all exposed surfaces down with an antibacterial solution. Then she takes her child's temperature, using one of those state-of-the-art thermometers that gently probe the ear canal.

Next, she calls the pediatrician for the best antibiotic available. He prescribes the latest thing—a nose spray so potent, it kills all strains of virus or bacteria.[4] The kid is given cherry-flavored Gatorade with electrolytes and sucks on Popsicles containing Tylenol. This isn't being sick, like I remember being sick. The kid's got it better than Ferris Bueller on his day off.

PLAYGROUNDS

Yesterday: The kids in my day did stuff that made our parents' hair stand on end. But fortunately, our parents were never around to see us doing it. That's because they were off doing incidental things like—oh, let's say—working.

We kids were real kids. We practiced stunts like hanging upside down from steel monkey bars, five feet above the ground. The only "net" below us was made of concrete. If I had taken a header on that stuff, I would have woken up in high school. No matter what

4. And nasal tissue.

the season, every sport would be considered "Xtreme" by today's standards.

In the winter, we piled three on top of each other on a sled[5] and raced down a hill covered with a pine tree obstacle course at 100 mph. In the summer, we dove into a swimming hole that was so polluted the fish had more genetic defects than a Hudson River trout. And guess what? We're still here. Darwin would've felt so validated.

Today: Recently, I took my grandkids to a park in Seattle. Taking stock of the place, I saw several things that totally amazed me. First of all, every piece of equipment is covered with child harnesses, safety straps, and restraints. Second, all the equipment is made from some soft material like Nerf balls. There are no sharp edges anywhere. Even the dirt and paved areas have been covered by three feet of spongy ground-up neoprene. It's impossible for a kid to get scratched or bruised or suffer anything more serious than a second-degree rubber burn.

The kids playing there wore helmets, kneepads, and chest protectors. I mean, the poor things could hardly move two inches, much less climb up a slide. A NASA space suit would have given them better flexibility. Both the moms and dads were there, directing their kids' every move. Each of them was protecting his kid by segregating them from the others on the basis of age, sex, and athletic ability. Wait a minute. Isn't this against the law?[6] Okay, at the risk of sounding like a fossil, I need an explanation here:

1. Why are the parents interfering with their kids' normal social interactions?
2. How can a kid learn anything if he doesn't have some older kid beating him up if he doesn't hand over his toys?
3. What were all those dads doing there on a weekday, anyway? Don't they have an office to go to?

5. Rosebud.
6. Technically, athletic apartheid.

DIET

Yesterday: Way back when, there were no rules about diet. Nothing was off-limits. We ate everything from the bottom of the food chain on up. Our parents believed that fat babies were happy babies. So, their mission was to fatten us up. Our moms didn't see anything wrong with feeding us solid foods[7] immediately after bringing us home from the hospital. We pigged out, plumped up, and everybody was happy.

Mom never worried about things like food allergies. In fact, no one even knew what they were. Back then, the medical treatment for just about anything was to ignore it until it went away by itself. Either that, or walk it off. If I broke out in hives or swelled up during dinner, Mom just threw me in a cold tub until I looked normal again.

Today: There have been so many restrictions put on kids' diets they practically aren't allowed to eat anything anymore. Parents have convinced themselves that their children's bad behavior is all due to food allergies. Nice try.

Most moms are positively obsessed about feeding their kids healthier foods. They scrutinize every label, choosing only those foods containing no salt, sugar, or additives.[8] Starting at birth, they're monitoring their child's cholesterol. And they have their kids counting fat grams even before they're potty-trained.

Today's moms are all about a nonfat lifestyle. And because they avoid carbs and fats like the plague, they're all super-skinny. They are convinced that this way of eating will make them healthier. Okay, I'll buy that.

But then they blow the whole theory by choosing role models like Calista Flockhart. Now, that's where I draw the line. Is this really their idea of healthy? A woman who weighs less than her Emmy?

---

7. Steaks, fries, and burgers.
8. And no taste.

Homeland Security

1. Which survival skill should be taught to all kids before they reach adulthood?
   a. making a fire
   b. purifying water
   c. building a shelter
   d. mixing a martini

2. Nowadays, what is the most popular item moms use when taking their toddler out for a stroll?
   a. an umbrella stroller
   b. a kiddie backpack
   c. the toddler trike
   d. a leash

3. In the '50s, people avoided getting into dangerous situations at parties where people were drinking too much by:
   a. staying home
   b. appointing a designated driver
   c. leaving early
   d. passing out

4. In the '50s, kids who took frequent car trips with their parents had:
   a. a bonding experience
   b. a desire to learn about nature
   c. a great time
   d. a death wish

5. The biggest threat to public safety in the '60s was:
   a. strontium 90
   b. the A-bomb
   c. mercury in the ocean
   d. Richard M. Nixon

6. In order to survive the Cold War, our parents learned the skill of:
   a. code deciphering
   b. sky watching
   c. wire tapping
   d. keg tapping

7. Our country's most tragic example of a species failing the survival of the fittest principle is:
   a. the bald eagle
   b. the carrier pigeon
   c. the whooping crane
   d. Richard Simmons

The answers to all of the above are d, as in "drink up."

Scoring:

1–3 correct: Grab the gusto.
4–7 correct: Grab a gun.

NINE

Shopping:
Change of a Dress

Here's an easy question for you. If a woman is given the choice between a night of wild, passionate sex or a President's Day 50 percent off sale, which one will she pick? That's a no-brainer. She'll choose shopping over sex anytime. It's a given. Women just love to shop—for anything. We make careers out of it. There is no high in the world like finding the perfect black dress or a pair of buttery soft leather pants that fit me like the paper on the wall. These are the things that can make me feel like a million bucks.[1]

As a rule, husbands hate it when their wives go shopping. Take my husband, for example. He sees it as a rivalry. First, he doesn't like me spending a lot of money. Second, he's jealous of the time it takes away from him. Third, it kills his ego when a $30.00 lacy bra can practically give me an orgasm.

But listen up. I've given him some advice that makes his life a lot easier. If my shopping doesn't make him happy, he fakes it.[2] When I excitedly tell him all about my shopping coups, he acts

1. Nearly costs it, too.
2. I do it all the time.

really enthused and interested. It's the fastest way into my good graces. If I get what I want, then he's going to get what he wants. It works. Here's a sample conversation I offered my husband as a guideline that will get him everywhere:

Wife: "Honey, look at this! I got this DKNY blazer for 30 percent off at Bloomie's. It only cost $388 on sale. Isn't it the greatest?"

Husband #1: The Wrong Reaction: "It cost $388 at 30 percent off? Are you nuts? Who do I look like—Mr. Moneybags?"

Husband #2: The Right Reaction: "Thirty percent off? Only $388 for that gorgeous thing? Wow! You're some smart shopper. Tell me more!"

Result: Sex vs. no sex that night. Guess which husband got lucky?

I rest my case.

Let's review the kinds of shopping excursions I like most:

The Shopping Safari—This is when I meet a group of women to take an all-day excursion to the outlet malls. This event isn't for amateurs, either. We have to be pros to pull off this kind of a trip. It takes split-second planning to make sure all the gals get what they want. Here's a typical agenda:

8:30 A.M.—Gals meet at a designated parking lot for carpool.

8:45–9:45 A.M.—Fortify our bodies with a *major-league breakfast* at Denny's. Stores we'd like to hit and shopping goals for the day are discussed over Belgian waffles. Burp.

10 A.M.—Arrive at the outlets. Park approximately 1.3 miles away from the stores in the humongous lot, the size of Rhode Island. Bottles of water and energy bars are distributed, providing our bodies with the requisite nourishment for the grueling day ahead.

10:15 A.M.—Strategy Session: The group splits up to cover as many stores as possible.

12 noon—We regroup for lunch. Drop purchases off in trunk of car. Recommendations on which stores are "musts." Compare notes on sale items.

1 P.M.—Off and shopping again. Part Deux.

3 P.M.—Meet at Starbucks for a decaf, low-fat mocha Frappuccino with a whisper of cinnamon. Show-and-tell time. Cell phones start ringing nonstop. Disgruntled family members are up in arms, demanding we come home.

6 P.M.—Shopped out. Our legs feel like rubber, our shoes are killing us, and our arms are aching from carrying seventy-five-pound shopping bags around. Despite the pain, we're deliriously happy with our purchases.

6:15 P.M.—Dinner at the Outback Steakhouse. We need meat. We need iron. We need a Bloomin' Onion, mate. Calls continue to pour in from irate husbands and whining kids. Gals review each other's purchases. Those experiencing buyer's remorse are quickly talked out of it.

7:30 P.M.—Home, sweet home. Enter to a level-three hostile environment. Even the pets are pissed.

8 P.M.—No worries, mate. Call the girls to plan next week's shopping trip.

Retail Sales—There is no enticement on earth stronger than these three words: 50 percent off. A great sale can motivate me to leave my sickbed for a few hours. And if the store offered an extra 20 percent off coupon on top of that, I might leave my deathbed!

I love sales as much as the next gal. But I admit, we women all fall into the same trap. We get brainwashed into this "sale mentality" thing. No matter what item is on the rack, if it says 70 percent off, we're buying it. Issues like, Do I need it? Does it fit? are irrelevant.

I'm one of those women who never learn. I have items in my closet that I bought on sale years ago and still haven't worn. I have purchased dozens of separates that don't match. I've got clothes that are too big or too small. I bought them only because they were on sale. The Fashion Police should arrest me for the following mistakes that have been hanging, unworn, in my closet for the past five years:

* The Purchase: A size two, white brocade Valentino gown with a matching ermine-trimmed cape. Cost: $899 at 40 percent off.
  The Problem: 1. I wear a size six. 2. There is no event I will ever attend in my natural lifetime where I could wear this ensemble.[3]

* The Purchase: A leather Ellen Tracy blazer. Cost: $250 at 30 percent off.
  The Problem: It's chartreuse. There has been nothing manufactured since the 1960s it will go with.

* The Purchase: A Christian Dior silk peignoir with ostrich feather trim. Cost: $109 at 75 percent off.
  The Problem: The last time I wore a getup like this to bed was on my first honeymoon in 1972.

* The Purchase: A full-length suede and shearling coat. Cost: $289 at 50 percent off.
  The Problem: In Los Angeles, where I live, there are only three days a year cold enough for me to wear it.

* The Purchase: A pair of stiletto-heeled, kidskin YSL boots. Cost: $209 at 60 percent off.
  The Problem: They kill me. I need to take four Extra-Strength Advil just to keep from screaming.

The High-Ticket Store—My girlfriend Catherine took me to a store in Beverly Hills called Buccellati, where they sell fabulously

---

3. Other than a coronation.

expensive jewelry. They also sell objets d'art, which is another name for stuff you couldn't possibly afford. This place is so exclusive, they keep the doors locked. We rang a bell, and an ultra-chic salesgirl let us in. Good thing Catherine was with me, because had I been alone, I never would have gotten past the guard. It would have been a replay of the time I tried to get into Studio 54 and got shot down at the door.

But Catherine is a beautiful society-type gal, with the style and pedigree[4] to get us in there.

This place had almost nothing "out" on the display shelves to see. Instead, the clients are given color sheets to peruse, featuring one-of-a-kind pieces of jewelry. After looking them over, you're supposed to request certain pieces be brought out to you. Well, la-di-freakin'-dah. Was I a long way from Wal-Mart or what? We saw quite a few items, but the one thing I didn't see was a price tag. Horror of horrors. That's so déclassé. Prices are given "on request." However, I'm sure the real reason behind this practice is that it would certainly cause somebody like me to go into cardiac arrest.

But I quickly learned to play the game, pretending:

* I knew who the designers were.
* I could afford them.

Catherine did most of the talking. She instantly bonded with the elegant salesgirl. They had so much in common . . . namely, Gucci leather pants and six-carat diamond rings. She was the real McCoy. I, but a mere poseur, trying to fit in.

When Catherine inquired about a bracelet by Michelangelo or somebody like that, I did catch the words "one hundred thousand." Omigod. That was just too much for me. I got weak in the knees. I asked the guard to let me out of the store. Then I made an emergency trip to Wal-Mart just to stop hyperventilating.

---

4. And required inoculations.

Discount Stores—Now, these are my kind of stores. The places where I feel the most at home. Places where the dressing rooms are a piece of cloth thrown over a clothesline. Where the floors are cement, and the fluorescent lighting makes me look like I've got hepatitis C. Yup. That's me. I love it. I welcome the challenge of:

* Trying to find anything in my size.
* Trying to find anything with a price tag on it.
* Trying not to faint without air conditioning on a 98-degree day.
* Trying to find a salesperson to wait on me.
* Trying to find the store, located in some back alley, miles from civilization.

Kmart—This store deserves honorable mention, because it's the mother and father of all discount stores. That's why it's hard to believe this place is in danger of going under. Frankly, I don't think it'll ever happen. All it would take to save the whole chain is for Martha Stewart to crack open her piggy bank.

Anyway, I love to shop here because it's got everything you can think of under one roof. But I have to be honest with you. The main reason I shop here is that it's a big ego booster for me. Every time I go in there and look around, I say to myself:

"I am the best looking person in this place."

and

"I'm also the richest."

You think that's out of line? Aw, don't go getting all politically correct on me. After the ego bruising I took at Buccellati, I need this place so I can look at myself in the mirror again.

Change of a Dress

1. When you're broke, the only way to shop is with:
    a. a credit card
    b. a gift certificate
    c. a line of credit
    d. Winona Ryder

2. The religion of most female shoppers is:
    a. Scientology
    b. Fundamentalism
    c. Christian Science
    d. Christan Dior

3. Which item sold by the cubic foot at Costco is the best bargain in the store?
    a. an air conditioner
    b. Styrofoam
    c. insulation
    d. lasagna

4. What's the first thing a woman does with all her purchases after she returns from a shopping spree?
    a. admires them
    b. tries them on
    c. hangs them in her closet
    d. hides them from her husband

5. The most common result of a three-day shopping binge is:
   a. buyer's remorse
   b. exhilaration
   c. fatigue
   d. divorce

6. What's the most popular name found on the tags at a discount store?
   a. Gloria Vanderbilt
   b. Jaclyn Smith
   c. Tommy Hilfiger
   d. irregular

7. Thanks to a big sale, your husband will be the only man in his office wearing:
   a. a Giorgio Armani suit
   b. a Rolex watch
   c. Burberry slacks
   d. lederhosen

The answers to all of the above are d, as in "deep discount."

Scoring:

1–3 correct: Go to blue-blood specialty shops.
4–7 correct: Go to blue-light specials.

TEN

Feeling Secure:
It All Depends

It's a basic part of a woman's nature to try and make the world a safer place to live. This is especially true of women who are moms. We spend most of our lives watching over our kids while they're sleeping, playing, or eating. No matter what they're doing, we keep a close eye on them. We all issue the same fundamental warnings, which our kids have followed since time began. These rules were written in stone and carried down the mountain by a Biblical figure like Ralph Nader. This was serious stuff, by Ralph. Obeying any of the following could potentially save your life:

THE RULE	THE RESULT
Don't run with scissors.	You could put your eye out.
Don't swim after eating.	You might drown.
Look both ways before crossing the street.	You might get hit by a car.
Don't play with matches.	You might get badly burned.
Don't have sex before you get married.	Your father will kill you.

OPERATION ENDURING SAFETY

They say most accidents occur at home. I know this to be true, because I have two sons to prove it. But that's only part of the story. After our kids are born, we moms go a little nutty making their environment as safe as possible. And in an age when all those high-tech gadgets are available, moms are making their homes more secure than ever. Many have done it so well they've turned their homes into fortresses. We're talking maximum-security facilities. Rikers has nothing on them.

I can't think of a better example of a childproofed environment than my son Michael's house. He and his wife, Whitney, have shown exceptional skill in this area, safeguarding their house for Sarah, three, and Joseph, one. There is nothing in the house that hasn't been altered in some way to make it safer for the kids. Now, don't get me wrong. I think it's a great idea. But I do have one teeny-weeny problem. Although their home is totally safe for kids, it's the most dangerous place on earth for an unsuspecting adult like me.

I recently visited them for a week and nearly didn't survive.

Here is how I spent my time, falling into one childproof booby trap after another:

The First Night—I get up in the middle of the night to go to the bathroom, and trip over the child's gate at the bottom of the stairs. I take a little spill, cutting my leg on the sharp edge of the latch. So now, I need a Band-Aid. But I can't figure out how to open the childproof lock on the medicine cabinet. So, I sit there, dabbing the cut with a Kleenex. When it begins throbbing, I figure I'd better take a Tylenol for the pain. But wouldn't you know it? I can't open the childproof cap on the bottle. I hobble out to the utility room, looking for a wrench to pry the sucker open. However, Michael's toolbox is rigged with a spring-release latch that bruises my knuckle. Count me among the walking wounded. But I still have to pee. So, I run into the bathroom and sit down hard on the john, without looking.

Oops. Add a bruised butt to the list. I am sitting on top of a little plastic potty seat that fits inside the regular seat. Ouch. At this rate, I better get back to bed, while I'm still able to walk.

The Next Day—During the afternoon, we decide to take the kids out for a little jaunt. The usual route is a stop at Costco, lunch at Red Robin, and then Toys "R" Us. I am excited about the prospect of spending the day with my grandchildren. But when I try getting into the back of the car with the kids—whoa!! Their regulation, state-approved child safety carriers are taking up 95 percent of the backseat. I am left with a four-inch strip of space to squeeze my middle-aged butt into.

Somehow, I manage to cram in between the kids, thinking I will just grin and bear it for the thirty-minute ride. At least I have some floor room to stretch out my legs. Scratch that. Whitney proceeds to load up every square centimeter of available space with tote bags. They contain items essential for surviving the thirty-minute ride. One tote is packed with diapers, bottles, juice, toys, and crayons. Another contains dozens of Ziploc bags filled with Cheerios, sliced apples, string cheese, and assorted cookies.

Whew. The cramped quarters are really getting to me. I start sweating profusely, feeling like a sardine back there.[1] I am close to suffocation as it is, then add the panic attack I'm having from claustrophobia . . . and watch out! I feel the overwhelming urge to flee. Luckily, I catch a break. Michael hasn't started the engine yet. So, I lunge for the door. Foiled again. It's locked from the front control panel on the driver's side. Pant . . . pant. I'm having difficulty catching a break. Let me outta here. Now, I'm in the midst of a full-blown, heart-palpitating panic attack.

I've got to replace some of the sugar I'm burning up at warp speed. So I grab Sarah's sipping cup and chug down the Hi-C fruit punch containing 99.9 percent sugar. Then I grab Joseph's stash of

---

1. I smelled like one, too.

M&M's and crunch away. After a few minutes, the panicky feeling starts to subside. It is replaced by nausea. At least it's the lesser of two evils. I need a distraction. By the 154th chorus of "I Love You, You Love Me" from the Barney CD, I think I've got one.

That Night—After we get back home, I decide to lie down for a while. After all, it's been twenty years since I've been around kids. I'm not used to all the noise, the crying, and being stared at for six hours straight. At my age, I need my solitude. So, I am thankful to lie down for a while in my grandson's room. But, when I look up from my pillow, I see my sorry face on the baby TV monitor staring back at me. Good God. That's a fright. It's Big Brother 2002. I guess I'm just not ready for all of this. In order to prepare myself for the next visit, I think I'll go to a halfway house first.

AIRPORT SECURITY: AN OXYMORON

You know what occurred to me? Since women are so good at this security stuff, why limit our talent to our homes and kids? Why not branch out into the realm of national security? Historically, we have left our safety in the charge of men, and look where that's gotten us. Lord knows, the world has been a total mess for centuries. And now, every time you turn around, our country is being put on high alert.[2] Danger lurks around every corner. In fact, it's become so dangerous to live in this country that all the illegal aliens are sneaking back over the border to go home.

So what would women do to make the country safer? Well, the first thing I'd do is revamp the whole airport security system. The way it stands now, men have turned our airports into chaos. It's ridiculous. We have to show up two days before our flights. A total overhaul is necessary, starting with the curbside check-in.

As it is, the minute I step onto the curb for check-in, I get

---

2. By Dick Cheney from an undisclosed location.

barraged with idiotic questions. Questions designed to act as a deterrent to terrorists. Shut up. Big deterrent. Like some terrorist is going to answer them truthfully. Get a life.

I think that stupid questions deserve stupid answers. This is how I feel like answering:

> Q: Did you pack your bags yourself?
>
> A: No, I always ask a stranger to do it for me.
>
> Q: Have your bags been in your possession all the time?
>
> A: No, I dropped them off at the corner of Hollywood and Vine for a few hours.
>
> Q: Did anyone give you something to carry on the plane?
>
> A: Yes. I'm carrying a bottle of Jack Daniel's and a bottle of Prozac.
>
> Q: Do you have anything to declare?
>
> A: Yes. I think you're an idiot.

Geez Louise. After that interview, I think the world would be a lot safer without these guys. If men really knew anything about security, they'd forget about the luggage. The first thing they should check is my purse. That's where some of the country's most lethal weapons are routinely stored:

ITEM	POTENTIAL USE
Nail file	As a biologist, I am capable of dissecting a human body with it.
Toothpicks	When shoved under his fingernails, a man will spill his guts.
Nail polish	Produces coma from toxic fumes
Mascara wand	Can permanently blind an attacker[3]
Curling iron	Can inflict third-degree burns

---

3. And give him full, thick lashes, too.

In any woman's hands, these items could maim or put a terrorist out of business. Besides my handbag, I routinely pass through security checkpoints wearing objects of mass destruction. Who needs a shoe bomb, when I'm wearing three-inch steel, stiletto high heels? What about my panty hose? They can be used to securely bind the hands of two terrorists.[4] Not to mention my underwire bra. It can do a better job of strangling somebody than one of Tony Soprano's henchmen.

OPERATION BOUNTY HUNTING

No doubt about it. If we had sent an army of women to Afghanistan, the war would be over by now. I mean, what are they thinking there in Washington? Here they have our entire military, the CIA, and Barney, the White House dog, sniffing out Bin Laden. And none of them have been successful yet. Then, what about their final act of desperation—sending Geraldo over there? Give me a break. This guy couldn't even find his way out of the Al Capone vault scam. So what did they expect him to do for this country—take out Bin Laden with a bomb concealed in his mustache? Not in this lifetime, buckaroo. About the only thing he caused was another scandal. During his second week over there, they discovered he was lying about his whereabouts. Big shock. He was supposed to be reporting from one place but was actually found in another. My guess would be the makeup trailer.

However, when the government put a $25 million price tag on Bin Laden's head—now that was really smart. But they didn't take it far enough. They need to send a woman in to finish a man's job. Actually, two women. Send Ivana Trump and Anna Nicole Smith over there. With a $25 million bounty at stake, those two gold-diggers will find the guy in a New York second.

---

4. Queen size can handle four.

It All Depends

1. Which objects most commonly set off the metal detectors at LAX airport?
   a. scissors
   b. tweezers
   c. metal lipstick case
   d. buns of steel

2. Which of the following is a good reason to put the country on high alert?
   a. terrorist threat
   b. impending storm
   c. missile attack
   d. Mike Tyson without Prozac

3. Chaining the Taliban prisoners to their seats on United Airlines while denying them food is called:
   a. detainment
   b. military containment
   c. prisoner control
   d. coach

4. What did the United States invent that qualifies as a weapon of mass destruction?
   a. nuclear bomb
   b. chemical warfare
   c. IBM missile
   d. Diaper Genie

5. What is the only thing left that all airlines will still guarantee?
   a. onboard safety
   b. good service
   c. an on-time arrival
   d. losing your luggage

6. The world lost one of the most brilliant minds in the Clinton administration with the passing of:
   a. Vince Foster
   b. James McDougal
   c. Senator Strom Thurmond
   d. Buddy, the White House dog

7. Who would be the best person to negotiate with terrorists?
   a. Jimmy Carter
   b. Abba Eban
   c. Henry Kissinger
   d. Dr. Phil

The answers to all of the following are d, as in "Dubya."

Scoring:

1–3 correct: Flying high.
4–7 correct: Hijacked.

ELEVEN

Technology: Do You Yahoo?

When it comes to keeping up with technology, I'm stuck somewhere between the Ice Age and the Stone Age. How bad is that? Byte me. I'm on hold while the rest of the world is whizzing by. Whew. All this self-flagellation has led to me to a personal catharsis. I feel the need to confess. To purge myself of this dirty little secret I've been carrying for years:

I am still writing my books on WordPerfect 5.1. Oh God, I said it. Oh-oh. Get the cyber smelling salts! I know you smart-alecky techies have just about gone comatose upon hearing this news. Give me a break. I can't help it. There's a reason I'm decades behind the rest of the world. In a word: fear.

The reason I'm not learning the latest program or using any new equipment is that I'm afraid of screwing everything up. When it comes to learning anything new, I have no confidence in myself. Trying to learn how to operate a new gadget or master a new program is just too much work! It's like having to study for a final exam again. So instead of moving forward, I'm stuck back in the '50s with my hi-fi. Oh, sure. Some people try to be PC and all when dealing with me. Like my son Michael. Whenever I call him long distance in a total panic because I erased something from the screen, he's always so patient:

"Mom—get a life! When the heck are you going to learn Windows? Even Sarah uses it, and she's only three years old!"

Gee, thanks for the compassion, Michael. I know how old my granddaughter is. I also know how pitiful I am. But, just in case I forgot, it was good of you to remind me.

However, my editor, Kelly, is another story. She's a woman, and therefore much more supportive. The first time I sent her a finished manuscript on a WordPerfect 5.1 disk, she laughed for two days. But she did try really hard to find a computer old enough to read it. She even had it carbon dated. Disheartened by her own failure, she e-mailed me this message:

"Jan. I haven't seen one of these disks since college."

Oops. How long will it take me to move ahead and get with the program here? Don't ask. Probably never. Oh, I go through the motions. I bought a state-of-the-art notebook, with all the accoutrements. I even keep it in a chic Burberry carrying case. I'm stylin' all right. The problem is, I'm not functioning. Here's my best excuse, and okay, I admit it's an excuse by default. I point the finger at my parents. If I'm stuck in the Stone Age, then by comparison, they're stuck in the primordial ooze of creation.

My folks are typical of all the over-seventy, Generation XXX parents, who still haven't learned to operate the VCR or DVD their kids gave them. For Pete's sake, it took me nearly ten years to persude them to get an answering machine. And now that they have one, they still haven't learned to use it. In fact, it nearly killed them. The day after they got it, I called their home and heard the following recorded greeting:

MOM: "No, no, Frank. Jan says you have to push *this* button."

DAD: "Betty, be quiet. You're supposed to push *this* one . . . hello . . . hello . . . helloooooo?"

MOM: "Frank, you're doing it all wrong. Push *this* one, dammit."

DAD: "Betty, you don't know what you're talking about. Let me do this . . . please. Hello? Testing . . . testing . . . testing . . ."

MOM: "Frank, you're being an idiot."

MOM: "Frank, put down the gun . . . Frank! . . . Beep."

Okay. I stuck in that last line for comic relief. But believe me, they came pretty close to homicide over that thing. And they're not alone. All my friends have to record messages for their parents. It's practically the law. So when it comes to buying presents for holidays or birthdays, just stick to the basics. Forget the VCRs, DVDs, computers, Palm Pilots, and other high-tech gadgets. They'll never take them out of the boxes. The following items found in your parents' homes are what they consider high-tech:

hand-operated eggbeater
nonelectric can opener
window air-conditioning unit
black-and-white Philco TV
rabbit ears
record player with fat attachment for 45s
1953 toaster[1]
plug-in metal coffee pot

Sure, maybe I am only a step removed from them. But there are a few things I learned that are invaluable for my everyday survival. I am the first to admit that all the new cyber aids are a blessing. However, like anything else, there is a flip side. They can be a curse, too. Here are some of the downsides:

1. With one setting—burnt.

Voice Mail: When you call a company, you never reach a real person. Here you are, bursting with questions and you can't even speak to anybody. What's up with that? How come they don't have anyone there to talk with you? These companies must make a practice of hiring employees who are either deceased or in a coma.

It's nothing but a hassle from the minute you're connected. The second your call goes through, they begin jerking you around. First, you're forced to listen to the dreaded option menu. From there on, it's all downhill. Like, when you call your bank with a question about your account, you get a series of recordings that go something like this:

- ✳ "If you want to hear this message in English, press one."
  Are you kidding me, lady? Who am I . . . Charo?
- ✳ "Enter the last four digits of your social security number, now."
  Give me a break. I can't even remember my birthdate.
- ✳ "Press two to access your balance."
- ✳ "Press three to report a change in address."
- ✳ "Press four for instructions about opening a credit line."
- ✳ "Press the pound sign and stay on the line to speak with an account representative."
  Lord, help me. I don't have the years to spare.

The good news: After you wait an eternity, a live[2] woman finally comes on the line. The bad news: She's got a raging case of PMS and a really snotty attitude. You haggle with this bee-atch for an hour, and then she says in a sarcastic tone . . . "Just what is it I can *do* for you?"

At this point, about the only appropriate thing to say is, "Just give me the number for the Suicide Hotline."

---

2. Or possibly cyborg.

E-mail: This is a service I learned my way around fast. I needed it for professional reasons. As an author, there's nothing like the intellectual thrill I get when I download jokes, send jpeg photos, write letters, and forward a bunch of spam to everyone I know. Just the other day, I forwarded some professional photographs[3] of my granddaughter to everybody in my address book. I am hooked. I even check my e-mail at 2 A.M. on my way to the bathroom. When I hear that familiar sexy voice, saying "You've got mail," I practically wet my pants.

E-mailing is so trendy. Nowadays, it's chic to put an e in front of everything. Everybody is in on the act. There are sites for ecommerce, eshopping, eloans, and edivorce. You can send e-mail from your cell phone, your Blackberry, and your Palm Pilot. It's so cool. Even when I log on to iron my clothes, I hear "You've got mail."

It's all about immediate gratification. We live in an instant society. Now we've added instant mail to all the other instant things we have enjoyed for years, like instant divorces. We have become accustomed to reaching whomever we want, whenever we want. And no matter how trivial our thoughts, we feel compelled to express them to somebody else within a nanosecond.

E-mail has changed the way America communicates. The post office is fast becoming obsolete. Even second-day airmail seems painfully slow now. Snail mail is unthinkable. Nobody wants to stand in line for forty-five minutes at the post office anymore. Besides, with all their stressed-out employees shooting up the place, you have a greater chance of losing your life than your mail.[4]

Cell Phones: The question is, how the heck did we ever manage to live without them? Really. It's hard to comprehend the mixed-up, messy life we must have led prior to them. Can you imagine driving in your car and not being able to call ahead for directions? Or to

---

3. Sonogram pictures.
4. 99-to-1 odds.

let your husband know you're going to be late? Or tracking down your kids' whereabouts after school?

I admit I am among the millions who have become totally cell-phone dependent. Yes, I am a cell phone junkie. Forget a twelve-step program. It wouldn't help. It would take years of deprogramming[5] to get me to give up this habit. Just the other day, I left the house without tucking my cell into my purse. When I realized I left it at home, you know what I did? I panicked. Yep. I had a full-blown anxiety attack right on the spot.

I know it's crazy. But my cell phone abuse is fueled by my need for reassurance. Self-indulgent? You bet. I even have the 5,000-minute-a-month plan, because of my neurotic need to reach out and touch everyone. I find it helps all areas of my life to work better:

Family—I call from the driveway to see if anybody is home.

PR—If I spot a friend dining in the same restaurant, I'll call her from four tables away to say hello.

Research—I call the library to find out important facts for my books, like the name of the presidential dog.

Marriage—I call my husband in his study to tell him dinner is on the table.

Voice Recognition: Nowadays, technology allows us to program our phones, computers, and cars to recognize voice commands. You only have to recite a name, like Sally, and your phone automatically dials her number. When you speak to your dashboard and say, "Radio—640 AM," it immediately tunes to that station. You can dictate letters to your computer, and it types out the words, correctly spelled, as you're saying them. Far out.

I love this voice recognition stuff, because it fulfills my need for constant conversation. It's reassuring to know that even if the whole world is mad at me, I can always talk to my appliances.

5. By the Moonies.

YOU'VE GOT A FRIEND

There are a lot of lonely people out there who are searching for some better meaning to life. Everybody is looking for a cause. A raison d'etre, if you will. Women often become advocates for the homeless, for children, and for animal rights. However, nine out of ten men agree the most pressing cause for them is obscenity— they're all for it. In fact, they are so dedicated that they're up all night pursuing this lofty goal. And what better place than the Internet to fulfill their dreams?

Thousands of seedy porno sites are just a click away, for all those lonely guys who have nothing better to do, like go to work. Web sites with names like www.nakedgirls4you.com or www.wevegotjugs.com get millions of hits per hour. This is where men feel most accepted, finding lots of male camaraderie out there. There is comfort in the fact that no matter what kind of a sick, twisted sexual deviate they are, they've got millions of pals online. Hey, guys. Go take a cold shower.

Viruses: These are diabolical things, which you must constantly be on the alert for. Our computers have become filing cabinets for everything in our lives. So, if a virus destroys all the files on a person's computer, it can throw them into a deep depression. Let's face it. When your hard drive crashes, it's worse than crashing your BMW. You practically have to hold a funeral.

Here are some of the deadly viruses going around the net I want to alert all my readers to:

Viagra Virus: freezes up your hard drive for four hours.

Al Gore Virus: causes your computer to just keep counting and counting.

Enron Virus: locates all your financial files and shreds them.

Bob Dole Virus: makes a new hard drive out of an old floppy.

Mike Tyson Virus: quits after two bytes.

Jack Kevorkian Virus: deletes all old files.

Lorena Bobbitt Virus: reformats the hard drive into a 3.5-inch floppy—then discards it.

Arnold Schwarzenegger Virus: terminates all files.

Do You Yahoo?

1. What room do 99 percent of all Americans spend their spare time in?
   a. bedroom
   b. family room
   c. dining room
   d. chat room

2. The most recent technological advance that was installed in my parents' home is:
   a. DSL cable
   b. satellite dish
   c. cordless phone
   d. indoor plumbing

3. Many doctors log on to which Web site for the latest in medical findings?
   a. NIH.gov
   b. BostonMedicalCenter.com
   c. HarvardMedicalSchool.edu
   d. NaughtyNurses.com

4. The best incentive to entice a man to hook up the DVD player is:
   a. an easy manual
   b. no installation charge
   c. no monthly charge
   d. *Debbie Does Dallas*

5. A tip-off your daughter is leading a promiscuous life is when she:
   a. stays out all night
   b. takes birth control pills
   c. takes drugs
   d. has her own Web site

6. The *69 technology offered by the phone companies has been an invaluable tool for:
   a. telemarketers
   b. large businesses
   c. credit companies
   d. suspicious wives

7. The best way to get rid of annoying telemarketers is to:
   a. block their calls
   b. hang up
   c. don't answer after 6 P.M.
   d. give them your mother-in-law's number

The answers to all of the above are d, as in "DSL."

Scoring:

1–3 correct: You've got RAM.
4–7 correct: You've got SPAM.

TWELVE

L.A.:
The Shallow End
of the Gene Pool

Whenever I mention that I live in L.A., the gals immediately perk up. Everybody wants to know what it's like to live out here in LaLa land. Is the population really made up of hedonistic, immature, and self-absorbed people? How insulting is that? Okay, so maybe we are. But what of it? What's so bad about being the feel-good capital of America? Somebody's got to do it.

Here's the top five questions people always ask me about L.A.:

1. Are the people really as shallow as they say?
2. Does everybody over forty automatically get a face-lift?
3. Do nine out of ten marriages end in divorce?
4. Are breast implants required by state law?
5. Would we elect Gary Condit as the leader of the Moral Majority?

Wow. These are tough, thought-provoking questions. Give me a minute. The answers are complex and require a lot of thought:

yes

yes

yes

yes

and yes

The truth is that L.A. proudly represents these things and much, much more. Sure, L.A. is a fake community. That's why I fit in. But, the cool thing is that there's always something exciting and trendy happening here. Like saying "cool" to describe everything. Who wouldn't get seduced by the glitz and glamour out here? I admit I did. So, what about it? Shoot me with a spandex bow and arrow.

I have lived in L.A. for twelve years. I think that gives me enough time to make intelligent comments about life in this city. Wow. Time flies when you're having fun. Twelve years in L.A. is like dog years—it's actually eighty-four in any other city. We live life in the fast lane. Everything out here seems to be for show, not longevity. Even implants only last ten years. But, in general, life is great in the land where the sun always shines.[1] Got sunblock?

Besides the glorious weather, the thing that sets this city apart from all the others is that this is where most of the movie stars live. It's a heady feeling to be having a drink at the Polo Lounge and look up to see Sharon Stone passing by your table. Even after twelve years, I still get excited when I spot a celebrity. It's still the same old thrill, every time I get blown off after requesting an autograph.

I know L.A. doesn't have a skyline as impressive as New York City. Our tallest structure is a statue of Mickey Mouse at the entrance to Disneyland. But we're tall in star power. We've got star maps, star delis, star-studded events, and psychics to the stars.

Here's my take on life in L.A.:

Trendy Coffee: In my dissertation on L.A., I would be remiss not

1. With a UV level of ten.

to include my thoughts on Starbucks. After all, it has become an integral part of the American landscape. In fact, a new one appears every week on some corner in every town in America. I'm not sure how this happens, but it must have something to do with secret government cloning. There's just no other explanation.

My relationship with Starbucks is complicated. It's the classic love/hate psychological scenario. I am inextricably drawn there, because I love the:

* Smell of coffee and cinnamon wafting in the air
* Chocolate chip scones
* Whipped cream on the lattes
* French vanilla decaf
* Ceramic coffee pots they sell for $60

On the other hand, I hate:

* Anyone who uses more than six words to order a coffee
* The gal ahead of me who orders those complicated drinks, which take an hour to make, for her entire office
* That the cost of one iced mocha Frappuccino is approaching the GNP
* The lines in the morning, which are longer than Yanni's hair extensions
* That after eating only three chocolate-covered coffee beans, I will be awake for the next ninety-six hours
* The coffee snobs who can taste the difference between Ethiopian and Sumatran blends, and hold a thirty-minute discussion about it

But the coolest thing about an L.A. Starbucks is that the guy in the corner wearing sunglasses, sipping a nonfat latte, who looks like George Clooney, *is* George Clooney. Forget about lusting over all those pastries in the display cabinet. I'm looking at the most delicious buns in town.

Trendy Restaurants: We've got plenty of those. What I know about trendy restaurants in L.A. can be summed up in one word: arugula. When did this happen? Every hot restaurant in L.A. features this item on the menu in one form or another. And if you're not eating it for every course, you're hopelessly unhip.

My beef about trendy restaurants is just that—where's the beef? Out here, everybody is so health conscious, the only things they dare serve patrons are organically grown veggies or field greens, swimming in balsamic vinaigrette. Shut up. This isn't dining— it's grazing.

It's also the "in thing" to call the food "haute cuisine." Translated this means "minuscule portions." I don't know about you, but when I'm paying $30 for an entrée, I want to leave feeling full. Every time my husband and I leave one of these restaurants, we're not only $150 poorer but we're also starving! We usually end up at the McDonald's drive-thru, ordering Big Macs and fries just to maintain our unhealthy cholesterol levels.

I think these establishments are aware of this. That's why they offer the complimentary after-dinner drink. It's usually some horrific thing like grappa, which is Italian for gasoline. They must figure that if they get us totally loaded, we'll forget how hungry we are.

Trendy Clubs: In L.A., you name it, they've got it. Whatever floats your boat. When it comes to naked dancing girls, this city is a latter day Sodom and Gomorrah. But heaven forbid they admit it. Instead, the strip joints try to come off as legitimate by referring to themselves as "high-class gentlemen's clubs." Translation: Booby Bistros. Oh, please. They're so transparent.[2] The term "classy" is used to mask all the voyeuristic antics going on in there. But don't forget, we're talking about guys here. Men consider dancing a legitimate art form only when it includes a pole.

But, for the rest of the population, they've got lots of legitimate

---

2. Like the showgirls' costumes.

dance clubs like the Roxy or the Key Club. The newest craze is the Latin Salsa clubs. Talk about hot. Chile peppers have nothing on them. Watching young people perform those wild dances like salsa and the Lambada is awesome. The steps are so intricate it must take years of practice to dance as well as they do. The kids are incredibly coordinated, and their movements are fluid. I don't think I could ever manage to move like they do. You've got to have hips on rollers. There's more gyrating happening in one night than in Elvis's entire career.

However, there's always a downside. The newspapers are filled with sensational stories about illegal drugs being sold at dance clubs. Apparently, Ecstasy, roofies, GHB, and coke are rampant in many of these establishments. To be honest, I've never seen it. But keep in mind the places I frequent are a lot tamer by comparison than the "in" places like the Viper Room. I go where they feature rock 'n' roll from the '50s—for those *in* their fifties. About the only thing I ever saw that was even close to an illegal substance was a middle-aged woman snorting St. John's Wort in the ladies' room.

Trendy Gyms: Warning: L.A. gyms are not for weaklings or the undisciplined. First of all, these places are packed at 3 A.M. That ought to tell you something. What? Darned if I know—but it definitely means something.

Here's what I do know. No matter what kind of cutting-edge equipment is invented to punish the human body, it's installed in an L.A. gym within twenty-four hours. Have you ever seen those macho looking chairs that have resistance weights on the arm and leg bars?[3] Ugh. These things look way too much like a birthing chair for me to be comfortable with.[4]

I usually pass these up in favor of the more wussy, softer equipment. I like those big European exercise balls you can flop down on and roll around all over the gym floor. The biggest advantage of

3. Manufactured in Qatar.
4. Twice as painful, too.

these is that you don't have to stand during the entire class. Now, that's my idea of a great workout.

However, the best reason to work out in an L.A. gym is the celebrities. When I want to see stars, I go to an L.A. gym.[5] All the movie stars are relentlessly working toward the same career goal: washboard abs. You might see Stallone huffing and puffing on the Stairmaster, or Jean-Claude Van Damme kick boxing on the aerobics deck, or Zsa Zsa in the weight room, bench-pressing her ten-carat diamond ring.[6]

Trendy Schools: The star factor has invaded all walks of life out here, and education hasn't been spared. Even the high-priced private schools in L.A. can be summed up in a word: star driven. I see it on the news. You never know who you're going to find roaming the halls of academia. You might encounter Michelle Pfeiffer reading to a second-grade class, or one of Cher's boyfriends working on a project in his junior high shop class.

The colleges are also caught up in the cinematic curricula. Many offer unconventional courses like a full semester of studying all the *I Love Lucy* episodes. Students regularly hand in Ph.D. dissertations analyzing movies like *It's a Wonderful Life.* Always mindful of their mentors, many film students carry an 8 x 10 glossy of their academic hero, Steven Spielberg, in their press kits. Most of the students do everything possible to emulate him. It's common to see a bunch of Spielberg clones walking around campus, wearing the same hairstyle, beard,[7] and glasses.

I got a clear picture of where American education is heading,[8] just by watching Jay Leno interviewing college kids on some of the campuses around L.A. Most of these kids don't have a clue that France is a country, much less where it's located. But they are able

---

5. Or drop a dumbbell on my head.
6. From a recliner.
7. Women, too.
8. Into the toilet.

to recall every plot of *Gilligan's Island* for a seven-year period. If he questions them about Turkey, they'll tell him it's one of the four food groups. And when asked to name two of our most famous astronauts, they'll say Major Healy and Tony Nelson. Oh boy, Houston. We've got a mega-problem.

Trendy Traffic: Okay, so traffic isn't trendy. But our discussion of L.A. would be incomplete without traffic talk. At any given hour in the day, our freeways are experiencing total chaos. We've got major congestion and gridlock going on all day long. However, the city has taken some measures to try and alleviate the problems by creating special "carpool lanes." Basically, these are lanes I can drive in only if I have more than one person in my car.

I, for one, think this is an unfair practice. It discriminates against the antisocial. Kind of a vehicular apartheid, if you will. It's a bad feeling to be alone in my car, stuck in traffic, only to look over into the carpool lane and see a group of more popular people whizzing by.

But still it's worth the hassle, because when we're driving, we've got something to look at that nobody else in the country has. Celebrities. If you're cruising in Beverly Hills, you might see Tom Cruise-ing around in his Jag . . . using cruise control . . . with a Cruz sitting next to him. One afternoon I spotted Jay Leno on the 405, zooming along in one of his cool hot rods. And one night in front of Spago, I came close to backing into an Aston Martin driven by Mr. 007 himself, Pierce Brosnan. Close call. I was shaken . . . not stirred, though.

Watching movie stars makes driving a lot more interesting and fun. It's sure a whole lot better than doing the usual boring thing— like watching the road.

The Shallow End of the Gene Pool

1. The most traveled lane on an L.A. freeway is the:
   a. outside lane
   b. exit ramps
   c. carpool lane
   d. illegal alien lane

2. Which show on TV best represents the population of L.A.:
   a. *Will & Grace*
   b. *Frasier*
   c. *Felicity*
   d. *Queer as Folk*

3. The oldest and best-preserved monument in L.A. is:
   a. La Brea tar pits
   b. city hall
   c. Grauman's Chinese Theatre
   d. Dick Clark

4. More movie stars are seen where in L.A. than any other place:
   a. Spago
   b. Rodeo Drive
   c. Sky Bar
   d. drug rehab center

5. The hottest selling items on the streets of Beverly Hills are:
    a. Prada bags
    b. Gucci sunglasses
    c. Rolex knockoffs
    d. breast implants

6. Fathering children outside of marriage in L.A. gets you:
    a. jail time
    b. financial penalties
    c. a bad reputation
    d. elected

7. Which patriotic celebrity has seen more action than anyone else in Hollywood:
    a. Audie Murphy
    b. Colonel Jimmy Stewart
    c. Elvis Presley
    d. Pamela Anderson

The answers to all of the above are d, as in
"drugs, dancing, and debauchery."

Scoring:

1–3 correct: Consider yourself hip.
4–7 correct: Consider hip replacement for yourself.

THIRTEEN

$\mathcal{R}$eproduction: Send in the Clones

Okay, everyone take your seats. It's time for a lesson in reproduction. Bear with me, ladies. Remember, I was a biology teacher, so every now and again I get the urge to hold a class. If I remember correctly, there are two types of reproduction—asexual and sexual. Hold your horse DNA . . . this just in. According to the New Age French geneticists, the Raelians, human cloning has been achieved in their institution.[1] So, this baby makes three.

Asexual reproduction is commonly found in the lower organisms. Many of them possess both male and female reproductive organs. Consequently, they are considered to be both male and female sexes at the same time. Like RuPaul. These lower forms of life have the capacity to reproduce themselves without sexual contact with another organism. They actually fertilize their own eggs with their own sperm. Now, that's what I call a home run. There are many more species in our modern world that also reproduce asexually in great numbers:

1. Definitely mental.

* amoebas
* sponges
* snails
* the Osmonds

There are other species that reproduce by an even simpler process. All the one-celled organisms reproduce themselves by a process called cellular fission. They grow until their cell wall can no longer contain their protoplasm, then they split apart, forming two separate organisms. I believe Luciano Pavarotti is on the verge of doing this, but at this point, it's just a hunch. As far as I'm concerned, that's the way to go. No muss, no fuss. No morning sickness, no water retention, no dangerous mood swings.

Other multicelled organisms in the lower animal kingdom have methods just as impressive. I don't know why we insist on calling it the Lower Kingdom, though. That's so elitist. I think these animals are pretty darn smart. Take the earthworm. It's got both male and female reproductive organs housed in one body. And when these organs are feeling really close and good about each other,[2] they fertilize themselves. Then the earthworm deposits its fertilized eggs in the soil. Voilà! You've got worm.

I like this idea. Look at me, I did it all by myself! It eliminates the time-consuming and often painful steps of dating, getting married, and breaking up. Not to mention the therapy bills. So, let's not underestimate it. I think these earthworms are on the right track.

Sexual reproduction is another story. It's a lot more complicated. This process not only involves the male and female reproductive cells, called zygotes, but also the organs that produce them, the ovaries and testes. Science has been studying the process for years, successfully unlocking many of its mysteries. But there are still many more that remain to be solved. However, in the past few

2. Or after a big fight with themselves.

years, we've come really close to cracking them. For the first time in history, we've been able to artificially create life outside of the human body. We've come a long way, baby.

Still, the scientists aren't telling us all they know. Take the seahorse, for instance—in my opinion, the smartest of them all. In this species, the male carries and gives birth to live young. Brilliant. The female deposits the eggs into a pouch on the front of the male. He carries those little suckers in there until he gets really big, about the size of the Reverend Jerry Falwell. Then the pouch experiences a series of contractions, like labor, and the babies are spewed out into the water.

This makes all kinds of sense to me. Just think about it. The male gets to experience labor and delivery, firsthand. That's a case where it is nice to fool Mother Nature. I think we need to pass more laws protecting this species. And if we ever decide to replace the eagle as our national symbol, I'm voting for the male seahorse.

Let's review what we know about sexual reproduction:

TEMPUS FUGIT

I must be honest here. Although I am a biology teacher, I am also a married woman. So what do I know about sex? Not much. But there are a few things I do know. I know that we humans have a limited window of time in which we can reproduce. Our biological clocks are ticking away, and medicine is attempting to reset them. The fact that women are getting married later in life makes it more urgent than ever for science to beat the biological clock.

So, modern medical research has thrown itself into studies about sex and reproduction. Researchers are working overtime, trying to create medicines and surgical procedures that extend the life of our sexual organs. By forty, we're racing against time—and time is winning the race.

THE STUDIES

In our high-tech age, couples are under a great deal of pressure and stress with their jobs. Young people are working longer hours and have less leisure time for sex. And when they do make the time, they aren't enjoying it like they should. This is a growing concern in our society. How do I know? Because every other day, there's a new study that reports about the failed sex lives of the Yuppies.

Recently there was a study from women reporting they only experience orgasms 60 percent of the time. Really? Two things immediately come to mind:

1. I didn't know you were supposed to report it.
2. Who do you report it to?

Here's a thought. Maybe if we did less reporting and more practicing this wouldn't be happening.

In the race against time, science is trying to figure out how to keep our female sexual organs young and functioning. Researchers are coming up with all kinds of technological procedures to get around our biological time clocks. One of these procedures is in vitro fertilization. If a woman's eggs are too old, she can have donor eggs and sperm fertilized in a test tube, then implanted in her uterus. The uterus is primed with hormones, so it can support the fetus for the full nine-month term.

But in order for this procedure to succeed, the uterus and vagina have to be in good shape. They have to be healthy and strong enough to carry a baby for nine months and then deliver it. That's why there has been so much attention placed on the vagina of late.

VAGINAL VALIDATION

The year 2000 was groundbreaking for the female species. It was the year that the vagina came out of the closet. And I for one, say it's about time. As an organ, the vagina will finally take its rightful place up there alongside of the liver and gall bladder. And, not only is the vagina out of the closet, we've just discovered it can talk, too. That's right. It has been the subject of a hit play, *The Vagina Monologues*, touring the country. This play is enlightening people everywhere about the real power of the vagina. It is confirming what women have always known: The vagina has a mind of its own.[3]

I can't tell you how much progress we've made. Years ago, no one gave the vagina a second thought. It was just too politically incorrect an organ to mention. When I was growing up, if I dared utter that word in front of my mother, she would have gone catatonic.

But now that vaginas are in, medicine has turned its attention to them. And plastic surgeons are right there on the cutting edge,[4] making sure all our vaginas are as aesthetically pleasing as the rest of our bodies. They have even invented a new procedure, called vaginal rejuvenation, which is supposed to tighten and strengthen the aging vagina. I'm all for it. Sounds like a good idea to me. I only have one question: How do you know when it starts looking old?

So, rest assured, ladies. We can boldly go into the future with our vaginas as tight as our faces. But are we going just a bit overboard in this quest for youth? I mean, is it really necessary to preserve myself so well that I look thirty when I'm really eighty-five? Who am I—Evita Perón?

CLONING

Sometimes, when a woman is infertile, even the best medical procedures can't help. Then there are times when the normal process of conception is impossible. But we don't have to hit the wall. We have just opened up a whole new avenue to get around

---

3. And an IQ of 180.
4. Pun intended.

these problems. It's revolutionary. It's brave new world stuff. It's called cloning.

Cloning is not going to be easy for us to accept. Right now, this procedure costs a fortune and presents many risks. Also, there has been a huge public outcry against it on moral, religious, and ethical grounds. The people in my generation and my parents' generation are especially vocal on these issues. Many feel it's a violation of God's laws. I must admit that a part of me feels this way, too. On many levels, growing a human being through artificial means just doesn't seem right. It's not the way nature intended. At least not the way my generation did it. What's wrong with doing it the old fashioned way—liquored up in a cheap motel? There is also a whole segment of the population that doesn't believe we really cloned an animal. Many think that Dolly, the cloned sheep, was a total hoax. This is healthy skepticism. We have always questioned what is real and what is myth. Like:

* The Loch Ness monster
* The 1969 lunar landing
* Elvis's death
* Area 51
* The G spot

However, there is an upside. They're not only going to try cloning people, but also individual organs. So, theoretically, if I lose an organ to disease, cloning makes it possible to grow a new one from my own cells. Just think of it. No more waiting for a transplant, no more exhausting searches for a tissue match, no more fear of organ rejection. And no more wasting time searching for a new liver on eBay.

In spite of the controversy, the research is moving ahead. Just this year, they cloned the first domestic pet, a house cat. They named her CC, for carbon copy.

Who are they? Well, private companies are springing up, with the sole purpose of financing these efforts. I recently read about one called the Genetic Savings & Clone. Groan. I did not make this name up, honest. Anyway, they will freeze pet DNA and keep it to make a future clone, like when your pet dies. But it isn't cheap. They charge $895 for cloning and $100 for storage.

Wow. This sounds a lot like what my fur coats go through. And speaking of furs, the ASPCA is going nuts over the idea of cloning pets, denouncing it as highly exploitive. But, as we all know, money makes the world go 'round. Apparently, it makes cyclotrons go 'round too. Leave it up to the baser side of humanity to milk a buck out of any lofty process. Just look at the Internet. I rest my case.

It's only a matter of time before companies get into the cloning biz full force. When this happens, we'll be forced to suffer through all their ad campaigns. It's not going to be long before I pick up some magazine and read:

* Can't perform sexually?
  Send in a clone to do a man's job.
* Need to lose thirty pounds and grow some hair before your reunion?
  Wow 'em with your class clone.
* Just got sentenced to twenty-five-to-life for a felony?
  If you did the crime, let your clone do the time.
* Can't face another family Thanksgiving?
  Let your clone take the heat so you can get out of the kitchen.

We're going to rewrite history, folks. It won't be long until the day arrives when the stork will become extinct. When the kids ask where they came from, you just may have to say the Genetic Savings & Clone. Groan.

Send in the Clones

1. Sex is the most beautiful, natural thing:
   a. God created
   b. when it's between two consenting adults
   c. without birth control
   d. money can buy

2. The worst modern day crime against humanity is:
   a. genocide
   b. cloning
   c. biological warfare
   d. PMS

3. The most expensive eggs in the world are:
   a. from royal parentage
   b. sold on eBay
   c. cultured in fertility labs
   d. Fabergé

4. Asexual reproduction has been demonstrated in humans by:
   a. cloning
   b. lab researchers
   c. in vitro procedures
   d. Rosie O'Donnell

5. Which genetic mutation has recently been in the news:
   a. two-headed frog
   b. conjoined twins
   c. six-toed man
   d. Ozzy Osbourne

6. The one necessary skill all potential parents should become proficient in is:
   a. Lamaze technique
   b. child CPR
   c. Heimlich maneuver
   d. defrosting

7. What is America's most famous product of cloning?
   a. Dolly, the sheep
   b. CC, the cat
   c. Lola, the llama
   d. *NSYNC/Backstreet Boys

The answers to all of the above are d, as in "Hello, Dolly!"

Scoring:

1–3 correct: Proud parents.
4–7 correct: Parents without partners.